# PERSIA
# IS MY HEART

PERSIA
IS MY HEART

# PERSIA
# IS
# MY
# HEART

TOLD BY

Najmeh Najafi TO Helen Hinckley

DECORATIONS BY NAJMEH

HARPER & ROW ✲ PUBLISHERS
NEW YORK, EVANSTON AND LONDON

Library of Congress catalog card number: 53-5377

# CONTENTS

✦

# CONTENTS

# MY COUNTRY: AN INTRODUCTION

SITTING in the college library bent over my book, *Constitutional History of the United States*, I look like any American school girl. Perhaps I am shorter and more slight than most Western girls, but my clothes are right for America—bobby socks, slim red skirt, white sweater. I turn the pages slowly, slowly. It is not that I find the history uninteresting; my eyes, accustomed to passing from right to left over very different characters, falter, turn back, crawl on again.

Really I am more interested in this history than any other member of my class. To the American students it is an account of their nation's past. To me it is the story of the present and future of my country. America's struggle to win autonomy, sovereignty, economic independence is the struggle in which my country has been engaged during my whole life time, a struggle which is still far from finished.

"I know your country," American friends tell me. "I love the rugs and carpets of Persia, bright with varying reds and blues and gold that never fade; completely beautiful with intricate and fluid design; thick and soft as velvet."

1

I, too, love the carpets; but I see little children sitting at the looms, their eyes prisoners to the design, their bodies, needing play, prisoners to the weaver's bench.

"I know Persia," others say, "because I have seen her inlays, her silver work, her bronzes, and her enamel work."

I see our artisans sitting cross-legged, straining their eyes in their poorly lighted quarters, working the unbelievably

Just a little something made by hand.

minute designs, spending days and weeks on one piece which will somewhere in the world have to compete with a factory-made article.

"Persia?" another asks. "Oh, you mean Iran! I have heard, of course, of Iranian oil."

"Yes, Iran," I say, though I do not like the name as well as Persia. Both are ancient names, and Iran is the more ancient. Iran means "Land of the Aryans" or, as some say, "Land of the Nobles." The name of Persia comes from Parsua, once a part of my country which engulfed the whole and gave to it the name.

I think I do not like the name Iran because our country was renamed as part of a conscious program to make the people think back on the glories of the past. There was the same conscious program in Italy under Mussolini and in Germany under Hitler. It seems to me that the way to walk forward into the future is not to have the eyes turned toward the past. How easily can one stumble if the head is turned one way while the feet walk the other.

In speaking of my country we must use both names. Who ever heard of Iranian carpets or of Persian oil?

There are others, more learned, perhaps, but not more wise, who say, "Of course, I know Persia. I know her proud names: Cyrus, Darius, Xerxes. I know from the Bible that the Persian kings sent the Jews who had been carried into captivity by the Babylonians back to Jerusalem to rebuild their cities, carrying their sacred vessels with them."

But while I think of the glorious days of my country, I remember, too, the periods between these glorious days. And thinking of our place in the modern world where we have been duped and dominated by other powers, I remember one evening when my nurse, Zarah, took my brother Mosen and me with her to visit her own family. In the kitchen of the little cottage the great, rough cat had caught a mouse. Instead of killing it she let it run an arm's length away then she pounced on it. Again she let it run, again she pounced. I cried for Zarah to come and take away the cat, but Mosen held me, laughing. He was not cruel but this was a game to him. I felt myself to be the poor befuddled mouse. Each time he thought he was free he ran his little heart out while the cat gathered herself for another spring.

Persia has long been like that befuddled mouse.

Soviet Russia stretches along the entire northern and northeastern frontier of modern Iran except for the space occupied by the contested waters of the Caspian Sea. India with Afghanistan lies on our east. It has been Russia and Great Britain with her interest in India and in our oil who have been most active in dominating my country; though under pressure of world war even the United States has been an invader. On Iran's west are Turkey, Iraq and across the Persian Gulf, Saudi Arabia. Turkey and Arabia in more remote times have also been invaders.

One day, after I had talked about my country to a group of people at the University of California in Los Angeles, one of my countrymen said, "Najmeh, why do you tell the bad things about our country? Why don't you speak of the— the carpets?"

But I must speak the good and the bad—the truth. My country needs people who will try to see the truth and speak it for her.

Persia is a land of strange contrasts. Wide boulevards like Avenue Shahriza, lined with expensive Western automobiles, slice through the narrow twisting bazaar-bordered streets of old Teheran. Women, dressed in the latest Hollywood and Paris styles, copy the away-from-home manners of Western women but return to homes where their husbands are undisputed masters and women are, as the Koran says, "fields to be ploughed." American dance music blares through the courts of ancient mosques. Some people ride in American Cadillacs while others drive camels; some eat the richest food while hundreds of starving beggars throng the city streets; every man longs for freedom, yet ninety per cent are bound by poverty. The far-reaching desert, the windswept plateaus, the quick-rising mountains with the pureness of snow on their heads and shoulders give a sense of freedom that I have never felt anywhere else, but in Persia this feeling is an illusion. Not only has my country been dominated by some European power since the time of Napoleon, but many of her people are slaves to outworn customs, others to misunderstood modern ways. And most seriously, the great majority of my people are slaves to a very small minority who do not understand, or who are greedy.

The question most often asked me by my school friends is, "When you have finished school will you go back to your country?"

"Of course," I answer.

Then, with incredulity, "You will?"

It seems strange to many of my American friends that I should want to leave America for a land east of Baghdad, east of the Euphrates River, east of the Tigris, east of the Persian Gulf.

A country tucked away in the center of Asia may seem remote, but to anyone who has been in the American Southwest there is much in Persia that would seem familiar. It is not that modern Iran is about the same size as Texas, New Mexico, Arizona, and California combined (628,000 square miles). It is not that our population is about equivalent to that of those four states (16,000,000 people). Rather one would feel the bracing air of the high plateaus; see similar mountain ranges, similar valleys where fruits and grains and grasses are produced by irrigation, similar vast stretches of empty desert land.

Our deserts are as sterile as the salt flats of western Utah; no plants, no animals, not even lizards or snakes. And they are much, much larger. I have heard that Dash-ti-Kavin and Dash-ti-Lut (Land of Lot), the triangular sand basin surrounded on all sides by mountains, is the largest wasteland in the world. To the south, in Dash-ti-Lut, there are salt marshes which might be the remains of prehistoric lakes. There are two roads that cross this vast desert. I, myself, have traveled the road that lies to the far north and leads from Teheran to the holy city of Meshed. I am a Moslem and most of the Moslem sacred shrines lie outside Persia—Mecca, Medina, Kerbela, Nejef. Meshed, where Imam Riza is buried, is within our boundaries and the long journey across the desert sand is part of the religious experience of a pilgrimage. When I went to Meshed I traveled by automobile. It must have been far more romantic to go by camel.

There is another crossing between the two deserts where the waste sand is girdled by encroaching hills. This road I have never traveled.

My home is in Teheran, the capital city. The natural setting of Teheran reminds me a great deal of Salt Lake City. It, like Salt Lake City, lies at the foot of a half circle of mountains. Give Salt Lake City just one turn to the left so that the high mountains, with gardens and trees green on their lower slopes and snow pinkish-white on their summits, lie to the north and the arid hills stretch away to the east and you have a perfect background of Teheran. We say "Persia has seven climates." The climate of Teheran is like Salt Lake City's, with a cold snowy winter, a green spring, a dry summer, and a brilliant autumn.

But the city itself is not at all like Salt Lake City. Perhaps it is a little like Boston, a little like San Francisco, more like the cities of Europe. But no. Persian cities are not really like any other cities in the world. Teheran, Tabriz, Isfahan, Meshed, Shiraz, Resht, and Hamadan are our large cities. Though for centuries they were connected only by camel caravan they are much alike. In all of them are gleaming turquoise domes that cover our mosques with indescribable beauty, graceful minarets, high vaulted gateways covered with faïence of intricate design, miles of arcaded streets which we call bazaars, and always great public gardens, cool with trees. Persians love trees. In Persia trees depend upon man and we say, "When man dies the tree dies."

One night my tall nephew, Ali, and I went to a party at Teheran's Officers' Club. Mother sent us in her automobile with the warning, "Telephone for the car before midnight. After midnight Hassan goes back to his wife and family."

The party was exciting so Ali and I stayed on, telling each other that we would call a taxi. At two we left, though the party was far from over. There were no taxis in sight and Ali and I started to walk. First I took off my high-heeled slippers. Still I was very tired. Finally I began to cry from weariness. Ali looked behind and before him. "Najmeh, no one will see. Climb on." He bent and lifted me "piggy-back." Dressed in an ankle-length dress of orchid tulle with my silver slippers clasped together by the straps hanging about my neck, I rode home in state through the quiet Persian night. Our cities are not lighted like yours; over us spread the deep blue of the sky pierced with the sharp light of a thousand stars.

Never before had I really seen Teheran.

My mother and my nurse had told me about the days when Teheran was a walled city with four great gates topped with tiled minarets from which each morning strings and drums and cymbals and the chanting voices of men greeted the new sun with music. Now the walls had disappeared and Teheran stretched out on every side, even climbing the hills as American cities do.

Down a wide new boulevard, walled with the flat faces

of modern business buildings, we went. The buildings seemed high to me then, four or five stories, perhaps. (In Teheran skyscraping office buildings are not needed as most professional men—doctors and dentists, for example—have suites in their own residences for the examination and treatment of their patients.) Then we cut through a long arcade of the bazaar where Teheran is much as it was hundreds of years ago. Here during the day artisans and merchants sit cross-legged in the stalls with little exhibits of wares at their feet.

Past the new, past the ancient; past splendor, past filth; past beggars dozing in the doorways, past the sleeping homes of the rich.

Lifting my eyes I studied the sky line against a sky slowly whitening with the rising moon. There were the slightly sloping roofs of the modern European buildings, the domes and minarets of ancient Persia.

Before this early morning ride I had taken my city for granted; now I saw in it the whole problem of Persia; the fusion of the old with the new to be accomplished without turbulence, without violence.

Somehow in the life of my people there is a deeply woven pattern of violence. An ever convenient manner of dealing with a political problem is to assassinate the leader whom one wishes to depose. Perhaps this is because power gained by violence must be preserved in the same manner. Perhaps it is because the great mass of people have no training, no opportunity to raise their political voice in any other manner.

Once when I was a very small child I heard the servants talking together of a big celebration. Later I heard the cook ask my mother if she would prepare the breakfast the next day while he took his wife to the execution. Of course I was eager to go. Such talk of rising at four to be at "the place" before sunrise; of the men who sold roasted potatoes hot from their bake carts; of the jostling crowds beating their hands and stomping their feet to keep warm in the early morning cool! Nothing was said of the gibbets awaiting those who were to be executed, of the poor people themselves, who would hang from those gibbets before the eyes of a holiday crowd.

Of course Mother would not let me go, and her firm refusal silenced all coaxing. Later, when I was grown and could have made my own choice I did not want to go to that place. In Persia they say, "A man who has seen another hang will not readily risk his own neck." But I do not think this is the real reason for the public execution. I will be glad when we have no more of these in my country.

I was born in a rapidly changing Iran. During my own lifetime my country has tried to drink at one swallow the civilization which Europe has taken at least six hundred years to develop. Sometimes I wish that I had been born before the 900 miles of railway crossed our country; before the 15,000 miles of highway, choked with American and European motor cars, linked city with city. It must have been romantic to see the camel caravans, with bridles and harnesses hung with turquoise and many bells to ward off the "evil eye." Yet if I had I would now be ten years married and subject to the will of my husband rather than studying in America with the dream of someday helping my country to be only beautiful, no longer tragic.

If one wearies of too much "progress" one can easily go where there is too little. In the villages the ways of the West have been scarcely felt at all. The farmer still breaks his back using the most primitive tools, his wife and children beside him in the field.

Almost a fourth of the Persian people are still nomads who feel even less than the villagers the pressure of Western ways. Our nomads are not like the usual nomads. They do move with the grass, they do pitch their black tents where their flocks can drink and graze, but still they are different. There are places in the world where herdsmen move from one oasis to another, seldom returning to the same spot. In Persia the move is up and down. They live in the valleys and on the plains in the winter and climb to the mountains in the summer.

People in America tell me that stock and sheep raisers in their country do much the same thing, moving to the high government ranges in the summer and back to the lower feeding areas in the winter. But in Persia the life is different. The Persian herdsmen do not go with their animals leaving their wives in town for the children to finish the school term, to attend church, to see each Friday a picture show. They take the whole family, even the children and the feeble old people, though they have to cross angry spring-rivers in lung-inflated sheepskin rafts.

These nomad tribes have always resisted central government. Each man is a person, worth as much as he can show he is worth. The nomadic life is important to my country's moral fiber because each man carries in his heart the seed of democracy. Persia has an everlasting frontier in its mountains, an everlasting fountain of freedom in the hearts of the mountain people.

There is always one question asked me about my country. "Is there caste in Persia as there is in India?"

I am proud to answer, "No. We have no caste." Social class, yes, but that is different, since a man may climb by his own effort from one class to another. Reza Shah himself rose from a private in the army to become Shah of Shahs. Syyid Khan began life in a Kurdish village, worked as a stable boy in Hamadan, saved money, studied abroad, and went back home to become one of Persia's greatest physicians, treating both rich and poor.

Yet the American way—"from rags to riches"—is not often possible in my country. Though every man has the will and ability and the right to make himself a happy life, too often he does not have the opportunity.

Once I was entertained at the home of a great lady in Teheran. Sitting there, a tea glass cupped in her ringed hands, she said, "God gives money to those who can take care of it."

I looked at her too-fat figure in the dress of finest Persian fabric, I looked at the room in which we sat, beautiful with ancient carpets and draperies, and I remembered that she was born to wealth, married to wealth. What if she had been born in the village? It is an accident that she is rich and another poor. It is an accident that opportunity comes to the few and is denied to the many.

Sitting in the college library with *Constitutional History of the United States* before me, I think of everything which I am reading in relation to the needs and problems of my own country. I am, at present, an American school girl. But even in America, Persia is my heart.

# 2

# MYSELF

I DO not remember my tall, blue-eyed, fair-haired father who died when I was very young. His handsome face looks out from pictures in my home. People say that my brother, Mosen, and my sister, Fahri, look very much like him; but still I can't bring the memory of my father out of the deep core of my mind.

I do not even remember his funeral or his burial at Nejef, a famous city where many prominent people are buried.

I think I remember the shining black coaches drawn by fine Arabian horses which often stopped at our home and disgorged men of great prominence who had come to consult with my father. But perhaps that is because I have seen these coaches and connect them in my mind with the days that my father was living.

I am sure that I remember the house where I was born, though we moved from it when I was three years old. It was very different from an American house as all ancient Persian dwelling places are.

Opening on the avenue was a wide courtyard, beautiful with flowers, especially roses, and with trees. The courtyard was in the shape of a **T** with wide-stretched arms. In the left arm of the **T** there was a pool and behind it wrought metal steps ran to a gallery on the second floor which overlooked the court and ran the length of the salon.

It is the salon which I remember best. The arched door from the gallery opened into a small reception room where people might wait for an audience. It was also the place for taking off the shoes. In Persia the carpets on the floor are not for wiping away sand and dust from the shoes. A great door opened from the reception room into the salon which was very large, probably thirty feet wide by fifty feet long. The walls were entirely of windows and mirrors. Both the windows and mirrors were not set in great panes of blankness, rather they were small pieces of differing shapes, set together according to Persian design. The floor was covered with a fine, closely sheared Persian carpet. The furniture? Around the edge of the room there was a continuous sofa about twelve inches from the floor, softly padded and upholstered in finest Persian materials. The back rest, attached to the wall, was also covered with Persian fabric. There was no other furniture. No other was necessary.

At the right of the reception room was my father's private library. For he was a scholar. He had been educated in Arabia, Egypt, and Europe and had been teacher and adviser to Sultan Ahmed Shah, the last of the Kajar kings. Of this library I have no special memory.

Across the court and up another flight of steps was the formal dining room. This room was just like the salon except smaller, with walls of mirrors and windows, with a radiant rich rug and with the low seat all around the walls. There were no table or chairs in the dining room. When dinner was served a beautiful hand-wrought cloth was spread upon the carpet. Many foods were placed upon the cloth and a man-servant at each end prepared plates heaped with food of the guests' choosing. If the dinner party were for women the servants, too, would be women.

On the right arm of the **T** on the same side as the salon but not at all connected with it were the quarters of the women and children. It is not the Persian way for men to be bothered with children.

In America I have seen the wife in a home without servants rise from the dinner table and say to her husband, "Remember this is my night to go to the college. Jacqueline will help you with the dishes, then she must practice her music. See to that. Be sure that Sammie has cod-liver oil." Then she will kiss her husband and put on her lipstick. Or if this is a night for pleasure and not for learning, she has more feeling for the husband and will say, "Darling, don't bother with the dishes. Just rinse and stack them."

American women would know how spoiled they are if they could visit a home in Persia where even the house is built to keep the confusion of a family away from the man's ears.

Across the court from the women's quarters was a large library. This I remember because it had been touched by foreign influences. Here there were chairs of finest carved wood, very ancient in design—maybe Chinese, I don't know—and the walls were painted with pictures of the glorious episodes in Persian history.

Under the salon was a reception room for entertaining the servants of important visitors, for when one man arrived in a coach it took a driver and two servants on behind to get him correctly in and out of the coach. Underneath the kitchen and servant quarters were lodgings for the horses.

Across the avenue there was a separate house for guests. Sometimes guests stayed several months, sometimes only overnight.

I do not know why my mother moved from this house. Probably it was too much work to manage such an establishment when it was no longer needed for official reasons. Probably she loved the ancient house of her father to which we moved. Most likely, I think, her grief over the death of her husband was greater in the house where he had been master. My father was nearly forty when he married a black-eyed little girl of twelve. At twelve my mother was both gay and gentle, childlike and mature, and she loved my father from the day of their marriage.

Our second home was near our first. It was built around a square court in the center of which was a fountain surrounded by a garden. On one side of the court was a salon with its reception room for removing shoes. In this room the carpets and draperies were Persian but the furniture was European. On another side were a dining room which had a table and chairs, rooms for my two brothers who were still at home, and an apartment for my mother.

It was in this apartment of my mother that I first learned about God and the importance of being clean before Him.

Just before sunrise Mother rose to prepare for the morning devotions. First she washed her face, then her right arm, then her left. Next she bowed her head and washed the part in her hair, then her right foot and leg, followed by her left. Over each part of her body she passed the water from the copper bowl, three times. Cleansed, she put a white band around her head entirely covering her hair. Finally she put on her semicircular white veil and pinned it under her chin.

At sunrise from all the minarets in the city came the beautiful voices of men and boys chanting, "Allah Akbar, Allah Akbar, Allah Akbar." These words mean, "We believe in one supreme God," and the singing of them is the call to prayer.

When Mother heard the call ringing through the city, she went to her personal shrine in one corner of her bedroom. Here, facing toward Mecca, she knelt before her sajadeh. The sajadeh, a beautiful piece of Persian material—not a rug really but a piece of tapestry wrought with metal and silk thread— is placed on the floor. A second piece of tapestry, smaller than the first, is placed corner-wise on the first. In the center of this tapestry is placed what we call a moher, an oblong dish with each end brought to a point which makes six sides. The long side is placed parallel with the body of the one who prays. In the dish is sacred sand brought from Cabella, sand marked with a special design. Beyond the moher is the taspi, a string of prayer beads, and beyond that the Koran, the sacred book of the Moslems. I watched, filled with awe, as Mother knelt there. I could not hear her words though I saw the moving of her lips. When she bowed her forehead to the floor I thought, Surely God will hear the prayers of my mother. She is so good, so beautiful. And I felt a warmth and sweetness through my entire body which I cannot describe except with the matter-of-fact words, "religious experience."

These early morning devotions Mother repeated twice more during the day, always looking toward Mecca, the most sacred shrine of the Moslems, always keeping her mind from touching any earthly worry or desire.

On the third side of our home was a large linen room, a sitting room for the family, and my room, occupied by me and my nurse. In my room Zarah, my nurse, had her own shrine and as soon as I was old enough to pray a little sajadeh was spread for me.

Under my room was the kitchen; under the salon a great cistern for storing water, because when water flowed it must be taken care of until needed; and under the rest of the house storage for fuel and such things.

It was in this very ancient house with the Western furniture that most of my memories of home life in Persia center.

There had been eight children in our family. I was the eighth. Two had died, my oldest brother was away from home and my sisters were married while I was still tiny. My older sister, Fahti, and her husband, Sank, lived always away from Teheran and we saw them only when they visited in our home or when I visited them. Fahti's son, Amir, was just my age. I loved him to come to my home. I romped with him, trying to imagine that I was indeed a boy and not a mere girl child. Fahti was sweet, much like my mother, with very dark eyes and smooth black hair. She had another son, Sijavish, who was just two years younger than Amir. Amir and I used to escape from him to play games of our own. We called him "baby" and it gave me a fine feeling to be, for a while, not the baby in the house.

My second sister, Fahri, is beautiful. Her hair is a gold-shining blond and her eyes not blue, not green, but something changing between. And what beautiful skin she has always had—like the skin in American magazines the color of rich milk. Fahri's husband, Ashbage, has always been someone special to me. Fahri is just ten years older than I but she was married when I was three. Her son, Ali, was born when I was four.

"You have a beautiful sister," everyone told me, looking at Fahri so tall and slender and golden. And I would look at myself in the mirror then go to my mother. "Mother, when you can have beauty in your family like the beauty of Fahri, why didn't you save some for me?"

"You are beautiful," Mother would comfort me.

I'd put out my lower lip and hold it tight to stop its quivering. "I am little and brown and skinny."

"You are exactly beautiful," my mother would say, kissing me. "Look at your eyes."

Then I would go back to the mirror and look at my eyes. Just eyes, I thought.

At the time that Fahri and Ashbage were married, her beauty was for him alone, and for the family and close friends. Every woman in Persia wore the veil to cover her face from the eyes of strangers. Then Shah Reza, who had deposed Sultan Ahmed Shah, abolished the veil. I do not remember how my mother and Zarah felt about changing this ancient custom. Perhaps they wore the same veil over the head but removed it from the face. But I remember Fahri, dressed in a beautiful black dress with a large black hat of lace and metal thread, standing at the back door of our home waiting for the courage to go out with her face uncovered. My brother, Jafa, and Ashbage were trying to push her out of the door and she was giggling and giggling, her lovely face rose-red. Mosen and I watched, our mouths open. How could we know how it would feel to go out without one's face covered when always one had been veiled?

"Leave her alone, boys," Mother begged. But to Fahri she said, "There is tomorrow and tomorrow and tomorrow. Perhaps night is the easiest time for the first going out."

And at last Fahri, still blush-red and nervous, went out with Ashbage. They were going to the theater. It must have been strange in the theater with all the women in the audience conscious of unaccustomed eyes on their faces!

My brothers Jafa and Mosen were at home as I was growing up. Jafa married when I was ten and Mosen when I was fifteen. There is no home where there is not children's quarreling, I think. Mosen was always teasing me. I loved my collection of little dolls, all made of candy, but colored and shapely and beautiful. When I began to find my dolls with their arms and legs gone and even sometimes without heads, I ran to my mother. She said to Mosen, "Don't bite Najmeh's dolls. Don't bite their arms, their legs, nor their heads!"

For a time my dolls lived peaceably; then one day when I took them out to admire them they had all grown very pale and very thin. What sickness had struck our house, I wondered, and I ran crying to Mother. "Are my dolls sick? Suddenly they are so skinny!" Mother knew the answer to that, too, but Mosen hadn't really disobeyed her. He hadn't bitten them; he had only worked them over with his tongue.

Sometimes Mother used the American way to get the quarreling out of the house. She sent Mosen and me to a moving picture show. She owned the buildings in which the theaters were located and the men who leased them from her had given orders that our family should enter free. But I think Mother would have paid a good price, and gladly, to have us out of the way for a while. With us she sent an old man who looked after Mosen as Zarah looked after me. That poor man! We could never decide what picture to see. Mosen always wanted to see the cowboy picture. I wanted the jungle picture with a beautiful blond girl always rescued by a most amazing man. Finally the old man would threaten to take us home and we would come to an agreement. Sometimes we went to the cowboy pictures but more often to the jungle. I think Mosen liked Tarzan as much as I did and put up his fight for the Westerns mostly to tease me.

Those wonderful pictures! At the side of the screen was a man who told the story of what was happening, and my country is a land of good storytellers. In our country we do not have popcorn but anyway we eat in the show. We go with a supply of dried watermelon seed. All over the place you can hear the crack of the shells between strong teeth, the little splutter of the lips as the shell is spit out. It takes a great many watermelon seeds to fill a stomach; so this cracking, spitting, chewing is a constant accompaniment to the storyteller's words.

There is in the show, too, the pungent smell of orange rinds, the sharp fragrance of apple, the lighter perfume of apricot and peach. Often Mosen and I took a supply of cookies since in the excitement of seeing Tarzan swing out of the enemies' grasp on a wisp of grapevine we could not keep our minds on cracking the seeds and swallowed them whole instead.

What strange ideas of the world we got from those American films!

At home there were always girls to play with, usually girls older than I, and they played at my house. I seldom played away from home. I think the reason that my home was the center of the neighborhood is that my mother was a kind lady who never said "don't." In some homes in America as well as in Persia, I've noticed, the mother is more particular about the house than she is about the happiness of the children. Her every word is "don't touch," "don't use," "don't bother." I had a little friend with a mother like that and I was always thankful that mine was different. She liked to have me where she could see and hear me and my friends were always given our home.

Although I had many friends and loved them, too, I liked best to be with my mother or Zarah.

I remember day after day tagging my mother about the house as she followed her usual routine. First was the morning devotion; after that breakfast. Breakfast at our house was sometimes prepared by my mother, more often by our cook. We ate tea, cheese, bread, eggs, butter, honey, and milk— none of the flat tasteless cereals of the West. I do not like eggs, which were usually served boiled, and objected to eating them. Mother thought an egg a day was absolutely essential. Every morning there was an argument about that daily egg.

At breakfast, too, was the best time for Mosen to start a quarrel with me. Mother would coax and command, trying to stop our bickering. Finally she would say, "I believe God gives me the patience to endure my children," and I, at least, would be ashamed.

After breakfast Mother sat on the top step of the flight that led down to the kitchen and talked with Ootah, the cook, about food for the day. She, like other women of position, could never go to market herself, but she watched the buying for our household with a careful eye. In these morning talks with Ootah she gave the market list, and when the servant who had been sent to market returned she checked on each item. If the cucumbers were long and thick instead of the length of a child's hand and slender, she'd hold one up and say, "Who bought cucumbers for the donkey? Even the donkey won't eat them!" She always questioned the price paid as well as examining the quality.

The thing that interested me most about the morning talks was the daily argument about what the family should eat.

"My lady," Ootah would say, "what do we eat today?"

"It is good to make polo and horisht."

"Polo and horisht?" Ootah would moan. "But my lady, to make polo takes several days, and horisht—! Why, we haven't chicken or lamb in the house suitable for horisht. By the time I go to market and return it will be past midday. Polo and horisht." He would shake his head and his voice would beg for pity.

"What shall we eat today?" Mother would ask.

"Aush?" Ootah would ask, his voice suddenly cheerful.

"Aush," Mother would agree.

The next day Mother would suggest aush and Ootah would insist on polo and horisht.

It did not matter to me who won these arguments. Everything that Ootah cooked was delicious.

Polo is rice, prepared in the Persian manner. Our rice is different from that purchased in America. Each kernel is longer and stronger. It does not break down when it is cooked, but grows puffy and tender. The rice is first washed in warm water, a little salt is added, and it is allowed to stand for a day or two depending upon the temperature. By this time it is fluffy and soft. It is added to boiling water and cooked for ten or twelve minutes, then drained and tossed with a little butter. A baking dish is prepared with butter and spices on the bottom; the rice is piled in lightly and covered with more butter and spice, then it is baked an hour in the oven.

*Horisht* is really our word for gravy—but such gravy! The principal ingredient is chicken, fried or steamed, or perhaps lamb, infrequently beef. We do not eat pork in Persia because the eating of pork is forbidden by the Koran.

While the meat is being cooked for the horisht the other ingredients are bubbling slowly on the back of the fire. Chopped onion, parsley, celery, first fried in oil until they are soft but not brown, then added to tomato sauce and water. After an hour of slow simmering the chicken or meat is added to the sauce and allowed to stand long enough to take on its delicious flavor. This is horisht, and served with polo it is the best tasting food in the world.

Or perhaps it is the best tasting next to *aush*. Aush is our word for soup. In it all the vegetables in the market are mingled in meat stock or water. The aush is thickened with rice and made more delicious with the addition of many tiny balls of expertly spiced meat.

Persians love raw vegetables and there is always a variety of vegetables and plenty of crisp, brightly colored salads. Our everyday dessert is fruit and melon. Even in the winter melon which has been stored in straw is available on the market. Cake we have for special occasions; we have cookies, too, sometimes, but the pie is unknown in Persia. For that I am glad.

It seems to me that Ootah was always very old; yet he did not die until I was nearly grown. He was brown, skinny, and fast moving, and although he never measured any ingredient in his cooking, everything he made was delicious. At his home he had a fat, helpless wife. It is our custom to allow the servants to carry home to their families exactly the same food that is served on the table. This wife of Ootah's ate as much of his wonderful cooking as did all our family put together.

Finally he died and another cook took his place. Poor wife of Ootah! She had never learned to make food. My mother sent her food daily from our home so that she could stay fat and lazy; but she complained that the food was not as good as Ootah prepared for her. We didn't think so, either, but she taught us a truth. You can never please a person once he is spoiled.

After the morning discussion with Ootah, Mother checked all the work of the house. I followed her from place to place as she decided what must be done and assigned someone to take care of the task. When this check was completed, she returned to her room for devotions which were completed just in time for dinner. We have dinner at noon and dinner in the evening, too. Never lunch or supper. In the winter when the children are in school, a servant comes from each household with a tray of warm food. There are no hot dogs, hamburgers, or sandwiches in the school child's diet.

After dinner all the family slept, and after the nap it was time to pray again. In the late afternoon Mother served tea to friends, went calling, or perhaps went to the bazaar. Dinner was served again at about nine. Frequently we ate at eight-thirty and friends would say, "You, too, are becoming Westernized. Eating at such an early hour!" Then to each other, "These people are like the birds."

The last thing at night Mother again performed her devotions. Each time she prayed she went through the whole ceremony of washing, of putting on the veil, and of kneeling before the moher on the sajadeh. With prayer, the house, and her children, Mother was always busy. From the time that I first remember, Ali, Fahri's son, was at our home much of the time, and later other grandchildren came constantly.

Sometimes, instead of shadowing Mother I stayed with Zarah. Kind woman! She was not beautiful, not what you would call an intelligent woman, but she had the kindest heart and the gentlest hands in the world. And besides that she had courage. She had two children, and was carrying a third when her husband died suddenly leaving her without a livelihood of any kind. With the shock of his death came the birth of her third child. The milk for this little baby came into her breasts but the child didn't live to suckle her. When she heard from a friend who had somehow learned that my mother was without milk for me, she came to our home and for two years she gave me milk. She left her own little boys in the care of their grandmother, and once or twice a week she visited them. Sometimes she took me with her on these visits, and I bridged the space between classes as easily as I walked down the avenue. Her boys didn't fight with me as Mosen did. Perhaps because to them I was something new. Instead they played with me and brought out their small treasures for me to admire. Their house could have been placed inside our salon, but it was clean-scrubbed and Zarah's coming with a basket of special food from our house always filled it with excitement and happiness. This Zarah with the shining eyes was very different from the quiet person that moved about our house. For us she mended, did simple sewing, helped with the ironing, or in times of pressure, with the washing; and no matter how busy she was she had time for my bumps and bruises. I remember waking early in the morning to see Zarah kneeling at her own shrine in my room, only her dark, serene face showing through from her coarse white veil.

In Persia there are no social castes. The son of my nurse could rise to any position in my country which he had the ability to reach; but still you can feel the difference in the classes. In my country, for example, the grocer is in the same class with the servant in the home; but the merchant of rugs belongs to a high class.

The farthest I ever went from home was to the house of my uncle. This brother of my mother's had a very sweet, very kind wife who loved children and had no children of her own. Often she would send her car for me and I would stay a day or two or even more with her. She never came in the car. She was a very religious woman who felt that she must obey the Koran; she must be veiled. When Reza Shah made wearing the veil against the law, she never again left her home except on moonless nights. Her husband and her home were her life. It was my aunt who first taught me my devotions. She bribed me to learn them, paying me in candy and cookies and fruits. Now I could kneel at my own little sajadeh and have words to say instead of imitating the gestures of Mother and Zarah.

This is a loose translation of the Arabic: "God has the earth and the heavens. He created the earth. Thank God for the earth. Show me the right way. Forgive me my mistakes and give me Thy Blessings."

It is confusing to me to translate the Arabic into English because in Arabic we do not call God He or She. Maybe It, but with a different sense from the English use of the word. It is not right, I think, to attribute sex to God so I do not know how to make the translation correctly.

As I grew older this young aunt coaxed me to spend more and more time at her home. She was short with very long, black, shiny hair; her face was pleasant—perhaps cute—and round, and she was sunny natured and fat. There was a softness of her when she took me close to her that was comforting and good. And she was very, very religious. Mostly she wore the black dress and head scarf of the ancient days. To people like my aunt and uncle, the laws of Reza which made Western dress take the place of ancient clothing made no difference. They did not oppose the law. They simply lived above it.

My aunt was a perfect housekeeper. She had servants, but still she did much of the work herself so that her home might be entirely clean. She did beautiful things with the needle and loved to have me sit beside her learning all the intricate stitches while I repeated the tenets of the Moslem faith.

A Moslem must:

1—Keep the fast. (No food is to be eaten between sunrise and sunset the whole month of Ramazon.)

2—Make the pilgrimage to Mecca at least once.

3—Pray (say the special devotion after washing the face and hands and feet) at least three times a day, maybe five, looking toward Mecca.

4—Bear witness to the Faith by saying often, "There is no God but God and Mohammed is his prophet."

5—Give alms—one fortieth of all one possesses.

She taught me the vajeb—things we must do to be rewarded in Paradise; the mohbah—things we ought to do to be rewarded in Paradise; the mostahab—things we can do or not do as we wish which will not change Paradise for us; the makruh —disapproved acts which are still not evil and not punished; and the haram—forbidden acts that bring punishment in the next world just as failure to do the vajeb will.

One day when I was about three I watched her sew, snipping with shining scissors. "I want scissors," I told her. But she said, "A needle you can have always, but scissors must come from your mother."

"Mother," I said some time later, "I want scissors."

"No scissors. You'd hurt yourself with scissors."

Then one day she saw me busily sewing a doll dress. "Did Zarah cut the dress for you?"

"I cut it myself."

"Najmeh," she said in her sternest voice, thinking I had sneaked scissors from Zarah or from her. But I showed her how I had cut it. With my teeth. People of Persia have excellent strong teeth, strong finger nails, strong hair. But even when teeth are sharp and strong, they don't make the handiest scissors in the world.

The next day my mother bought scissors, needles, and thimble for me and helped me to collect bits of cloth for my sewing. When I was four I went into business. I made dresses for the dolls of other little girls, charging them one cent each.

I loved to dress dolls, I loved to make homes for them. Though I had many dolls, my favorite of which was a cloth doll made by my mother, I never enjoyed mothering them. I never talked to them, fondled them, took them out for walks. Perhaps I have not the heart of a mother.

"She has a gift," people told my mother when they saw my sewing. Later my mother bought me a sewing machine. I remember Fahri said, "Why do you buy that sewing machine for Najmeh? Why do you let her do what she wishes? When I was a little girl you told me, 'Do this, Fahri, Do that!'"

My mother did not have words to explain. I knew what I must do and she allowed me to lead the way.

Another thing I enjoyed very much was dancing. In my country there are traditional dances just as in America there are well-known songs and poems. Many of our dances tell stories; some are survivals from a very ancient time, like the

Zoroastrian Dance of Fire. Some come from the Islamic in-fluence. At first I used to dance just as I felt; but later I learned the traditional dances, blending my emotion with the emotion of the dance story. In our dancing the movement of the hands tells special things. There is a language of motion, and people who know this language can interpret the story as well as if it were in spoken words. People in America who have seen me dance say, "Your hands are so graceful!" Hands must be grace-ful in order to be talking hands.

Often when my mother had guests she would call me in to dance. In Persia one dances for friends, to give them pleasure, or sometimes for a good cause—what you call in America a "benefit." It would not be appropriate for me to dance for money, to entertain strangers, to make a career. I know here in America entertainers are well thought of. Professional enter-tainers in my country are applauded but they do not belong to the upper classes.

Maybe one of our traditional dances will explain this. It is the story of a dancer who was loved by a prince. He could not marry her because she was a dancer; so she went away with a broken heart. Without her he could not be happy, so he found her and told her that he would give up being a prince in order to marry her. If there were a choice between the kingdom and her he had made that choice. But she knew that he must be a prince and later a king for the good of his people, so she told him that her broken heart had been healed by another and that she no longer loved him.

So I danced for my mother's guests, but I had no ambition to be a dancer.

Often I sang to myself and soon I was singing for my mother's guests. I had lessons in the dance but never any lessons in singing. In Persia we have in our music what you call modes. We sing not only in your half steps and whole steps, but in quarter steps and eighth steps as well. We write our music, now, on the staves as you do, but the singer, herself, must alter the music as she sings, putting in the finer intervals. I have been told in America that the "intonation" in my singing is something like that in Oriental singing and very

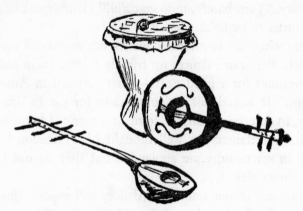

Instruments for making Persian music.

much like the quality of the American Indian voice. The song of the Peruvian priestess may sound very much like the song of the woman of Persia.

I love to sing. Even when I was a little child singing would carry me into an ecstasy and I'd change the tune according to the dictates of my emotions. Singing is a wide opening of the heart. Like dancing, it is a gift that is shared with friends. But I have never had ambition to be a singer.

All during my childhood my mother's cousin spent a part of her time in our home. We were instructed to call her cousin because she was as old as my mother. I gave her a new name, not to her face, of course: The Match. Persian matches are very thin. In your country you might call her "The Toothpick." I have never seen a thinner person except the so-skinny American movie stars. Maybe in America she would have been a great success in pictures. But her thinness was not her chief attraction for us. She had the gift of tale telling. Her stories were magic. We were willing to go to bed at five in the afternoon if she would tell a bedtime story.

With her stories we never grew sleepier, we grew more and more awake. As she finished a story we'd say, "And then what happened to her, Cousin?" and she would begin another.

I remember one night when she had told stories until she was hoarse we asked, "Then what happened to her, Cousin?"

She replied, "She died, she was murdered, she was cut into bits!"

"Mother," I wailed, "Mother!"

"No, I was wrong," The Match said, thinking very fast. "That didn't happen to her at all. What is wrong with me that I should make that mistake?" And quickly she talked until I hushed my crying to listen.

Her gift of words. That was the gift I wanted. When I was four or five I used to return from seeing a moving picture with Mosen and my older brother, Jafa, would pay me ten cents, even twenty cents for retelling the story to him. I liked the feeling of importance that his listening gave me. Someday, I hoped, people would listen to me and live in my words as we did in the words of The Match.

And so my life went. Loving my mother; feeling very close to my nurse, to my aunt, to The Match; scrapping with Mosen; admiring Jafa and Fahri and Fahti and Ashbage; playing with the older girls who lived near me; sewing, dancing, singing.

My life was bounded by the walls of our house and garden, by the adjacent streets, except for the excursions to the home of my aunt or the short calls to the home of Zarah.

I was a "baby," but the time was coming when I could know the bigger world of Teheran.

## · 3 ·

# HOLIDAYS AND HUNGER

AND then, almost abruptly, I was a baby no longer. I was seven years old, old enough to go more often to the home of my aunt and to the home of Zarah, old enough to get acquainted with more of the great city of Teheran, gazing at the displays in the bazaars, feeling the crowds of people around me, dropping coins into the hands of beggars. People! I found I loved them. I liked to be close mixed with the people, even though I did not know them. I was beginning to feel that I was not the center of the world; that the world has as many centers as it has people.

I was old enough, too, to join in the celebrations of my country. Celebrations like New Year's.

In Persia the new year begins with the spring as a new year should. When the days are beginning to lengthen, when the snow has receded to the top of Mt. Demavend, when the tree buds are bursting with flags of yellowish green, when everywhere the fragrant, purple violet lifts its wild little face— that is the time for the New Year.

We do not follow the calendar of the West. Because we

have lunar months, many holidays come at varying times as Easter does in your country. But always New Year's is the first day of spring. In my country the joy is so great when we say farewell to the used-up year and the used-up winter that we celebrate for three days.

In every home there is a party. According to the ancient custom there must be on the table seven things beginning with S. There can be many more foods, too, but the seven S's there must be. It is the custom to put on the table a bowl of goldfish to complete the number seven. There will be besides the goldfish, fruit, cake, several kinds of bread, olives (much saltier and more zesty than yours), fish, cheese, yogurt, sour cream, milk, eggs, salt, and delicious candy that looks like cheese but tastes like nothing in this world. I do not have the recipe for this candy, but it is made of sesame flour, sugar, and other things.

We must have the milk and eggs on the table always because they are basic to life. The beginning of life is the egg, life's early staff, the milk.

Even in the humble homes there will be seven S's spread upon the cloth, and in the homes of the rich much more besides.

There is giving of gifts, too. Everybody gives gifts to someone and it is the practice for the older to give gifts to the younger. The head of the house gives gifts to all. My mother gave to those who served exactly as to her guests. A very nice custom is that everybody receives a kiss when coming into the house. Kiss, kiss, kiss. But it is a very pleasant custom.

In each home the party is held just one night. The other two nights the family will be going from party to party in the homes of others. This is very exciting to a child who until yesterday was a baby and can now join for the first time in the festivities.

The Tuesday evening before New Year's the girls gather in little groups. Always in Persia it is boys in one group and girls in another. There is never the nice mixture that there is in the West. The girls giggle and whisper as they put on masks and veils. This is the night for the masquerade. It is like children trick-or-treating on Hallowe'en in America, only probably gayer since there are no dead people, skeletons, and ghosts, in the background. I do not specially remember my first exciting Tuesday evening because that memory is merged with those from other years.

After dark each girl from the giggling group takes a bowl and spoon. Before a neighbor's door the girls cluster, beating on the bowl with the spoon. The door is opened. The house-holder, jolly, happy, joking, invites the girls into the house. He and his family try to guess who the masked girls are. Into the bowls go money, fruit, candy, flowers, other gifts.

Those in the house make a wish and the girls say, "Yes, your wish will come true." Or, "No. So sorry. Very sad. Your wish will not come true." Then the one who has made the wish acts very glad or very sad, but it is all in fun. All the time the girls giggle and laugh and giggle again.

One evening I specially remember because a lady took my hand and turned it over, looking at it. "This is a clean hand," she said. "This hand never works. It is the hand of a lady." The next year when I went there with the girls this lady said, "This is the same hand I saw last year. The clean, lady hand."

Oh, it was a pleasure. The seven of us laughing until midnight, our shyness hidden behind a mask and a veil.

Then there are beautiful family customs, too. On the first

day of the year the family goes out into a field. There each person makes a chain of grass. For each blade of grass a good wish is made for the home and for the family.

Just before the new year the mother of the family makes a wheat cake. This is a very special unbaked cake and in it are whole grains of wheat. The wheat cake is in layers, one for each member of the family. I loved to watch my mother make this cake. "A cake for Jafa, a cake for Mosen, a cake for Najmeh," she would say. The unbaked cake is kept moist and soon the wheat begins to grow and the cake becomes a beautiful green thing. On the thirteenth day of the New Year (thirteen is a bad number in my country), the family takes this cake out into the fields and throws it away. With it go all the bad feelings, all the quarrelings in the home.

This is a pleasant custom. I hope maybe sometime I will make a cake for my children.

The last evening before the coming of the new year, silence settles over the celebration. This is the time for going to church. There are rich people in Persia who have copied American picture show ways, who drink and dance in the night clubs instead of going in for worship; but the real people do not forget God in looking toward the new year.

I remember so well that first night that I went to worship for the new year. In my hand I held a few grains of rice. Everyone holds in his hand either rice or wheat. These grains are basic to life, the very beginning of life, a symbol of fertility, of new life growing from old. In the other hand I carried the Book, my very own copy of the Koran. I was only beginning to read the Arabic in which the Koran is written, but I must do everything that my nurse and mother do.

As we entered the church we said a prayer. "God forgive me.

I am weak, I am humble, but I am trying. Please, God, give us rain, give us peace with our neighbors, give us freedom from sickness and sorrow." In the Moslem church everybody prays to God for himself. There is no distinction between black and white, between him who is a servant and him who is served, between him who is ruled and him who rules. God knows the value of each human heart and all men are brothers.

An important mullah.

We sat on the beautiful carpet on the floor of the church, the women on one side, the men on the other. With the women were the children, and I snuggled close between my mother and Zarah as I tried to follow the words of the *mullah* who spoke of the goodness of God and the kindness one man owes another. My eyes went to the pillars that held up the brilliantly colored domed ceiling. The pillars were of brick covered with colored tile in intricate and beautiful design, and my eyes followed these designs, half guessing what natural thing—bird, animal, flower—was subdued in the mind of the artist into this conventional pattern. But my heart responded to the beauty and even more than the words I heard my eyes carried to my heart the joy of a religious experience. Hanging from the ceiling were enormous chandeliers. There are electric lights in these chandeliers nowadays. I think I can remember when each glowed with one thousand candles, but I am not sure. I may remember the story of Zarah or of my mother.

We left the church when the new year had begun. Still we were praying in a secret way, "God, forgive my mistakes. I am trying in this new year. I am really trying." And because the spirit of the church was in the heart it seemed that if I tried all would be easy.

As we walked home, I stumbled a little because I was out much later than usual and because I did not look where I was going. I was looking up at the stars in the dome of the sky. Zarah said, "I am happy tonight. Nowhere in Persia is anyone hungry."

And I thought about hunger. Many times I had heard the beggars coax, "Give, please. I am hungry." But I knew nothing of hunger. I had never been hungry.

Now I was old enough to visit the palace of the Shah who receives all those who wish to call on the first day of the new year. I did not wish to see Shah Reza, a great giant of a man with eyes that frightened me, but I did wish to see the palace. With my mother I entered the garden through an arched gateway. There is a narrow strip of garden before the first court, the court of government offices. These are graceful buildings with galleries facing on the courts. The galleries reminded me of the one on our first home, except these are not open but curtained with silk.

We went through more arches, more passageways, into the central garden. The sunlight brightened the color of the flowers and of the faïence-covered walls of the buildings that surround the court. Beyond is the building where the Shah sits in state on the first day of the new year. The building is something like what you in America call a band shell, open at one side. In it is a carved throne surrounded by columns. On the floor is a rich carpet for the Shah to sit upon, his feet tucked under him.

Still farther is the palace itself, two-storied and many-windowed. I wanted to stay in the garden, watching the people, looking at the smooth grass, the early spring flowers, the fountains, the tiny streams running in blue tiled courses; but Mother drew me along and up the marble steps.

A tremendous wooden door was opened for us and we were in the throne room. It is a great vaulted room with polished floors and painted walls. There are deep alcoves with narrow windows. I caught my breath. The dream of Aladdin when he passed by the jewels in the underground room in order to reach the magic lamp might have been inspired by this room. Everywhere there are jewels. There are jewels on the shelves in the alcoves, thick sewn on the carpets which hang against the walls, festooned from the ceiling of the room down to the throne, displayed in glass cases down the center of the room. In one alcove there are swords sheathed in rubies, scepters set with turquoise and sapphire, diamond crowns, breast plates set with emeralds. There are rings, bracelets, glasses of unset jewels.

But the beauty of the jewels is at the same time fiery and cold. I caught my breath but my heart wasn't warmed. I wandered over to look at the display of enamel work. Here the colors were softly blended. The design reminded me of the pillars of the church. I lost myself in looking behind the design for God's creation that inspired it. It is against the Islamic religion to make pictures of the creations of God, but the design that suggests it and yet is a thing of beauty for itself is good.

"That is the Peacock Throne," Mother said. "It was brought from Delhi by Nadir Shah almost two hundred years ago." Obediently I looked at it. It is a blaze of gold and enamel and precious jewels. There are softly lustrous pearls sewn to the scarlet carpet on the floor of the throne. Yet to me the throne was not exactly beautiful. It was rich, yes, and dazzling and splendid. This is the heart of my country, and I was not happy to find it so fiery and so cold.

"It is a symbol of your country's greatness," Mother said. Perhaps I was too young to understand. I tugged at her hand. I wanted to be out in the garden again. As we went out we passed the guards. They were pleasant-looking men with no worries. One virtue of my country is that the people, although many are poor and hungry, will not take that which is not theirs. I tugged again at Mother's hand. I wished that I had the pure, warm feeling that I had as I left the church on the first hour of the new year.

Then life went on much as usual. I had celebrated New Year's, and I had, for the first time, been to the palace of the Shah. I began to think that being a child was not much different from being a baby. Still Mosen teased me, still Zarah slept on the floor near my half-size bed in my room, still I begged for stories from The Match.

Finally it was the eve of Mohammed's birthday. Mohammed's birthday is always on Friday, but because of our lunar calendar I cannot say what date it is. The celebration of the

prophet's birthday is to Moslems much as Thanksgiving is to
American Christians. "The earth is the Lord's and the fullness
thereof." To man, God gives. It is a custom in my country to
take barbecued lamb to the poor people so that all may share
in giving thanks.

Early Zarah spoke of this year taking the lamb to people in a
nearby village. At once I began to beg to go with her. "It is
good," Zarah counseled my mother. "Najmeh must know how
the people in the village live." Mother consented and I
watched the preparation of the lamb with unusual interest.

The whole lamb is purchased ready for cooking. It is placed
in an earthenware vessel over a very slow charcoal fire. With
it are water, tomato, onion, herbs. For a long time, six or eight
hours, it is cooked.

Late afternoon we went in the car to the village, maybe ten
miles, maybe twelve, from Teheran.

I had seen nothing in Teheran to prepare me for the village.
You have nothing in America to help you see it, unless it is the
Indian village of the American Southwest. In the old days each
of these villages was surrounded by a mud wall to keep the
sand out of the garden spots. Some villages still have these
walls. But this village near Teheran had no walls. First I saw
trees, poplar and cypress, then I saw the homes of the people.
The houses were clustered in the center of the village around
the home of the Kalandar—the headman. You might say in
English, sheriff, or maybe justice of the peace; I think you
haven't a real equivalent. He had a home with a large room
where he received the people. It was, perhaps, his office. Behind this room were rooms for his family and a kitchen. Ad-
joining on the other side was a room for his animals: oxen,
maybe a donkey, almost certainly a cow or goat.

This home looked very large in comparison with the other houses in the village, yet it was made of sun-dried brick—what you call adobe—and it had no windows. There were two doors which admitted the light and air that the sheriff needed.

The houses clustered about were made of the same brown sun-dried brick. They were mostly one-room houses, though some had an attached kitchen. In parts of Persia where there is no snow these huts are flat-roofed, but near Teheran the houses are dome-shaped which makes them very strong. There is no need to worry about a roof since the walls converge and form the top of the house. Only if a heavy rain comes are these houses threatened; then the water is absorbed by the dry earth and the house melts to the ground. It is not much loss, however. There is much free dirt, and houses are made from it. The new house may be built upon the mound formed by the collapsing of the old.

In the house there are no windows, just one door. If the weather is pleasant, the people sit in front of their houses doing work that requires the eyes; there is almost never light enough inside. These houses do not stand on regular streets, surrounded by gardens. They are huddled together and the farm lands outside the village stretch away as far as irrigation water can reach.

I clutched Zarah's hand as our driver helped us out of the car. The village was so strange, so ugly. The little children stared and the older people smiled. As the manservant who had come with us gave the gifts of meat, I peeked through the open door into the houses. Inside there was nothing. The people sat upon the floor, slept upon the floor, ate upon the floor. A few had rugs, some a samovar; but in most houses the only things of beauty were the copper kettles used to cook over the open fire.

But the people were beautiful, especially those that work hadn't robbed of their suppleness of body. There were shining hair, even white teeth, soft eyes. Too little food had made the fine bones of the face visible. Suddenly I wanted to reach out and touch these people. I felt that they belonged to me. I was happy as I had been when I touched shoulders with the people of Teheran, but this happiness was different. It was deeper and it carried pain.

When the lamb was all gone, Zarah and I got into the car again. Zarah sighed deeply; she was tired. But her voice was not tired when she said, "I thank God that there is no one hungry in Persia tonight."

These were the same words that she had spoken as I stumbled home from church between her and my mother, looking at the stars instead of the bricks under my feet.

But now I thought I was beginning to understand what she meant.

# MY LETTERS

A ND this old lady," said The Match, "wanted to travel more than she wanted to do anything else. She wanted to travel the wide world over. She had heard of—" Here the story could be lengthened by describing the wonders of the world that the old lady wanted to see until I was entertained for a whole evening; or it might be shortened to fill in the time before dinner by the abrupt phrase, "She had heard tales of many lands and of many people."

"Did she get her wish?" I would ask, although I had heard the story many times before.

"The old lady worked very, very hard. All her life she worked, thinking and dreaming of traveling. Each time she received a coin she put it away. And as the silver grew, the old lady's longing for travel grew. At last, one evening when she counted the pieces of money, she discovered she at last had enough. She hurried to get ready for the journey but her bones were old and her steps were slow and uncertain. 'Allah, Allah,' she said, 'I am seventy-five and seventy-five is too old for traveling.' And she put her face upon her carpet and wept.

"Finally she stood up. 'I will see the world. I must!' So she prayed to God and this is what she said: 'Oh, God, let me go traveling. Let me see many lands and many people.'"

"And did God give her her wish?" I'd ask, wanting to be reassured, even though I knew how the story ended.

"He sent a great bird who alighted at her front door. She climbed on the back of this bird and it carried her the wide world over. All in one night she saw the world. In the morning the great bird brought her back to her own door."

"Tell it again," I'd beg The Match as soon as she had finished. Already I could imagine that I was the old lady with my heart set on traveling and seeing "many lands and many people."

My mother had traveled, my father had been many places. I do not know why I didn't beg my mother to tell me of her childhood in Czarist Russia where her father represented Persia; or of my father's student days in Egypt and France and Turkey, and of his later travels throughout Europe and the Middle East with Ahmed Shah. It simply never occurred to me. Perhaps because in our home those years were in a locked box. I began to plan to see for myself what the "whole wide world" was like. Of course I was just a child, but the seeds of a dream were planted by the story told by The Match.

My greatest traveling in those days was down the avenue and across a few streets to the school.

I had been in school since I was five, but the school had not yet begun to broaden my life. It was like another room of my home with my teacher, Zarah, taking the place for a few hours of my nurse, Zarah.

Ordinarily children in Persia do not go to school until they are six. There are no kindergartens in connection with the public schools of our country. There are the ancient *mektabs*, Moslem schools, kept for little girls by old women whose faces are like withered apples, the fingers on their hands like winter-dead twigs; for the boys by old men.

Once when I was three, or maybe four, my mother sent me to such a school. She and Zarah were busy and it seemed a good idea. I remember that my mother gave me a book before she left me seated at the feet of the old lady. I don't remember much except that we were told to keep quiet. Some way I got

The teacher drowsed.

a pair of scissors and cut all the pictures out of my book while the mektab teacher drowsed. At noon we were served little wheat cakes for lunch, and after I had eaten I lay down on the carpet and slept. It was the time for my nap.

I do not remember whether I went to the mektab for two days or three.

When I was five one of my friends, a girl maybe two years older than I, maybe three, stopped at my house on the way to school. "Come along with me," she suggested. "No one will be angry."

"No one will be angry? They won't be angry at the school?" I asked, to make doubly certain before I made any decision.

Most American children would not understand why she told me, "No one will be angry." It is because in my country children live with fear. Parents, teachers, nearly everyone near the children are stern, frequently harsh; they expect and demand absolute obedience. The idea of a child having a need for self-expression, for self-realization, has never entered the adult mind. My own mother was kind, but even she believed that the mother should completely dominate the child.

In America I have seen a family, the father and mother and two little children, meet together in family council. The problem the four discussed was, "What can each of us do to increase the feeling of happiness in our home," and the little girl of six spoke as freely as the father. This we could never see in our country. The child giving suggestions to the father! That children can speak out in America is part, I think, of American democracy.

"No one will be angry," my friend again assured me, and I went with her to the school.

The school, like my home, was built on three sides of a rather large court. In the center of the court was a pool. The principal's office faced the court on the left side. The school principal was a woman with a harsh, almost manlike face whose duty it seemed to the little girls in the school was to make the law, accuse the offender, find her guilty, and punish her all in one quick action. My friend told me this in a quick whisper as we went around the other end of the pool to escape her chance attention.

At the other end of the pool the school janitors had the first room. It was a large supply closet, really, but they had stocked it with candy and other goodies which they sold to the girls for several times the price charged in the bazaars. I do not know how they got this concession, whether by purchase or "gift." They were nicknamed by the girls "Father" and "Mother." The rest of that wing and the building facing the court from the rear contained classrooms.

You ask about the lavatory? Listen, we are talking about Persia.

There was a small closet where the *aftabe* was kept. The aftabe is a rather large round jug with a narrow neck and a wide mouth. On one side is a spout, on the other side is a handle. The aftabe is for use if you need a rest room. After you have used it you carry it to the pool in the center of the court, empty it and wash it clean. That is what the pool is really for—for the emptying and washing of the aftabe.

We do not mind using the aftabe at school. We are all girls at the school, and besides we are used to the same system at home.

After my friend had shown me where the aftabe was kept, she took me to the first-grade room and I went in alone. No one asked, "Whose girl is this? What age is she?" I was given a seat with Nahede and Mastaneh, who today are two of my best friends, though we have gone different ways in life. Mastaneh is married and has a home and children. Nahede is a student in Teheran. Sitting there with the two little girls all day, I had a delicious sense of belonging.

Things weren't quite so smooth at home when I returned that afternoon, though. "Where have you been? Why did you go?" These were the questions. "You are too young for school—a baby," both Zarah and my mother said. Perhaps they were thinking of my three days at Mektab.

"But I want to go to school," I coaxed. The next morning my mother went with me and signed my name on the school records.

I sometimes wonder why I was so willing, even eager, to sit absolutely still for six hours a day, six days a week. There is no play in the schools of my country, and the only free day is Friday, the Moslem Sabbath.

There are six grades, equivalent to the eight grades in an American elementary school. The whole approach to learning is different. First there are the twenty-five letters of our alphabet that we must learn to recognize and recite in order. Next we must learn how these letters make words. Very soon we are given a book and begin to sound out the words and see them in sentences. The back of a Persian book is the front to an American. Starting on the last page we read each line from right to left. Many of the people of the West have told me that our letters look like the symbols in shorthand, but ours is a language like the Western languages in which a combination of letters makes a syllable and one or more syllables make a word.

As soon as we begin to master the reading of Farsi, the language of Persia, we must learn the Arabic since the Koran is written in that language and it is important that each person be able to read about her religion for herself. Arithmetic is another subject that Persians are particularly quick at learning. Omar Khayyám, the Persian poet that all English readers know, also wrote a book on algebra. The numbers we learn in school are similar to yours, since we too got them and our decimal system from the Arabs. There is never any time in the Persian elementary school for the drawing of pictures, the playing of games, the telling of stories, the singing of songs.

School is tiring for the body but it is refreshing to the mind. Have you seen a fish that has just been taken from the water with its mouth open reaching for air? My mind has always been like the fish's mouth—open for information and wisdom. When I finished the first grade my teacher, Zarah, advanced me to the third grade where I would be more evenly matched with the other children.

I did not know, as I went to school, that for every Persian village that has a school there are twenty-five that do not. I did not know that in all of Persia there are less than nine thousand schools and that only fifteen hundred of these are free public schools, the rest are private schools, many of which are mektabs. Yet I had the feeling that I was lucky to be learning.

The Mektab.

Often my favorite aunt sent her car to school for me on Thursday afternoon and kept me over Friday with her, sending me back to school on Saturday morning. During the school vacation she coaxed me to spend as much time with her as I could. She loved me as she had when I was tiny, but now there was a difference in our relationship. Before, she had been my teacher, showing me how to sew, listening to me repeat my devotions; now I was her teacher. Each word I learned to read and write I taught to her. She laughed with delight when I checked her small arithmetic problems and found them correct. She clapped her hands when she read a chapter in my primer without error. She had never had a chance to attend school and she was hungry for knowledge. Perhaps it was from her that I learned that there is a joy in learning that people who take education for granted may never find.

One day, I believe that I was in the third grade—or perhaps in the fourth—I saw upon the teacher's desk a globe with wide expanses of blue surrounding odd-shaped, vari-colored patches. All morning I kept my eyes upon the globe, waiting for an explanation. At last the teacher said, "We shall study geography. This globe stands for the world."

In a second I knew that all of the blue spaces were oceans and that the vari-colored areas were the "lands and people" that The Match had told about in her story. I could see the great bird winging its way around the globe and I decided with the little old lady in The Match's story, "I will travel. I must." First, of course, we found Persia; next our near neighbors; and finally, twirling the globe slowly, Western Europe and on the other side of a wide space of blue, America.

I do not know whether or not my teacher was particularly gifted in the teaching of geography. I know only that the subject captivated me; maps became my favorite possessions, and I followed every strange name, with the thought that some day I would see that place.

Because I dreamed always of travel, I kept my ears listening for talk about the Trans-Iranian Railway which was being built to connect the Persian Gulf with the Caspian Sea.

Although Mother had been born in this century, she could remember when all going and coming in Persia was by camel caravan or by coach drawn by swift Arabian horses. Sometimes we got her to tell of travel from caravansary to caravansary; of the uncertainty that went with travel because of the unfriendly tribes along the route, the robbers, and the roads that were sometimes really trails. She made this travel seem very romantic—much more interesting than riding in the foreign car behind our careful driver on the new roads that had been built in the time of Reza Shah.

And often the talk was of the new railroad that was to connect the Caspian Sea with the Persian Gulf. I did not know then that this 870-mile railway is the most remarkable in the world; that it passes from sea level over a 9,500 feet summit; that it crosses 4,102 bridges and passes through 224 tunnels, some of which turn several times inside the mountain; that in one place the railroad crosses six bridges and goes through four tunnels to travel nine hundred feet as the bird flies. There was little talk of these things. Both at home and on the street and at the bath I heard grumbling of how much the railroad was costing, grumbling that it was really a military road and did not reach out to the really important areas of the country, grumbling that the taxes to build the road were being paid by people who could least afford to pay them since much of the money was raised by taxes on tea and sugar, the two things that everyone, no matter how poor, must buy. Many who paid the tax would never ride the train, would never be served by the train in any way.

Sometimes whispers called the new railway Reza Shah's extravagance.

When I was seven the railway was completed. All of the school children of Teheran were invited to the celebration. The high school girls, dressed in white and with baskets of flowers, filled the great Teheran railway station. We young ones stood in the streets where we could see nothing of the celebration. We stood for hours. While there was music and

talking and more music and much more talking we stood
watching our wilting flowers and wondering if it would be
polite for us to sit on the pavement to rest a little.

Across the rails there was a band of ribbon. All of this crowd
was assembled to watch Reza Shah cut that ribbon. Of course
we didn't see a thing. I could imagine how it all looked,
though. Many times I had seen the Shah. He rode from place
to place in a big Rolls-Royce. Any time he might turn up anywhere to ask some official to give an accounting of himself. We
sometimes saw him pass in the street.

I had seen him at court occasions, too. A great, strong man
with a face that scared me. He was six feet three and he stood
straight as a poplar. His face looked closed, withdrawn, you
would say sullen. His eyes—they were the fearful feature.
Smoldering fire. He looked like a Cossack soldier, and that is
what he was. He had come to his position through his own personality, his own intelligence, his own drive.

His face and figure were familiar to everybody. There were
many statues of him in Teheran and his face and name were
on all of the new public buildings.

Even as we trudged back to school, the holiday spirit all
washed away by weariness, we heard people in the streets mut-
tering that taxes were fifteen times higher than they had been
under the old Shah. I did not care about taxes—then. I was
sorry not to have been close enough to see the first train
thunder from the Persian Gulf to the Caspian Sea. I was eager
to ride on that train.

About the time that geography was introduced to us, we also
began the study of history. Reading history was like listening
to The Match tell her endless stories. Only now the people
were real people, not men and women out of the mind alone.

For the first time I began to see my country in its real light: it had helped to cradle civilization. Many lands and people were somewhat different because of the greatness of the past Persia.

When I was ten or eleven I went on my first real journey. Ashbage and Mother were talking in the salon one afternoon when I came home from school. "It would be pleasure to have her with us," Ashbage was saying, and when I came in both his eyes and Mother's were on me.

"Would you like to go traveling?" Ashbage asked.

"Traveling!" I said, and I ran out of the salon and across the court to begin to lay out the clothes that I would need for a journey.

"You're a funny little thing," Ashbage said when he came and found me. "Do you know where we are going?"

"We are going. That is all," I said, and he laughed again.

He handed me a letter from my sister Fahti, inviting us to come to her home for a few days. "Fahri and I are going," he said. "We shall rent a car and you may go too."

"Zarah," I called. "Zarah!" And I sent her scurrying for a suitcase.

"Najmeh," Mother said, "you are going for just three days. You may put a clean cotton dress and your night things in Fahri's suitcase."

"I need a suitcase. I need many dresses," I told my mother, and Ashbage laughed and said, "There will be room for a suitcase."

"You spoil the child," my mother said.

For two days I packed and unpacked my suitcase, changing my mind hourly about what I should wear. With a strip of velvet I rubbed my shoes until they shone like a very black mirror. Zarah parted my hair straight down my head from front to back and put a pink bow on each side. Waiting for Ashbage and Fahri, I stood in front of the mirror thinking how everyone would say, "What a pretty girl goes traveling!"

But in the mirror was a skinny little girl with too big eyes looking half scared and half funny with the great ribbons on her head. Again I went to Mother. "What happened you make me skinny and small?"

Mother held me tight in her arms. "You have beauty," she said, and somehow I knew she was saying that to have me out of Teheran for three days would not make her truly happy. I did not want to decide to stay home, so I pulled away from her arms and went down the street to Fahri's house. She was all ready, but one thousand times she was telling the servants, "Don't forget this. Don't forget that. Put water on this flower. Remember this errand."

Ashbage came home in the shiny black rented car. "Come, Fahri," he begged.

"Just a minute until I speak to Mother." She hurried to the court of my home dragging little Ali so fast his feet were not often on the ground. "Here is Ali, Mother. Be a good boy, dear. Obey your grandmother." Then while Ashbage waited and I twisted with excitement, Fahri repeated every order she had made to the servants. "See that the servants do this. See that the servants do that."

"Yes, yes," Mother said often, very patiently, and soon Ashbage came into the house and pushing Fahri before him took her to the car. For a time I sat between them in the wide seat, then I moved over where my head could be propped on the side cushion and fell asleep. It was a five- or six-hour drive to the village where Sank was the Kalandar. Many times I wakened and slept. At last I sat up straight to see the road crossing many fields of melons. The melons that grow in Persia! They are not like your watermelons, but I do not mean the Persian melons that you buy in the markets of America. These melons are very long, like an arm, and so sweet and fresh and crisp. I used to think if someday I could be a millionaire I would buy so many of these melons that I would take just the first half-inch cut out of each melon. The first cut was so much sweeter than the rest of the melon. Now with melons on both sides of the road I thought I might have this happy future even without being a millionaire.

It was evening when we arrived at the home of Fahti and Sank. The two boys were waiting for me with bright eyes, but they were clean scrubbed, not ready for play. Dinner was already prepared in the big room of the home. The home was very large, and it seemed to me there were many servants; more servants than in my home in Teheran. Inside it was whitewashed and plain, but it was clean and the floors were covered with carpets of great beauty.

Even while we were eating, guests came to meet Fahti's sisters. "You have a very beautiful sister, Fahti," the friends said, but looking at Fahri dainty and fresh as if she had not been traveling much of the day. I knew they did not say, "Najmeh is beautiful."

For dinner there was melon—great, sweet slices. And I ate and ate. If Mother or Zarah had been there they would have put a hand on my arm, but Fahti and Fahri smiled at me and forgot me in the pleasure of being together. They were nearly the same age and had much to say about "Do you remember this?" and "Are you remembering that?"

Sank, round faced and jolly and very kind, finally said, "If we are going to the play—"

We said our devotions and got ready for the play. I was

beginning to feel very crowded inside from all of the melon, but I must see the play. For a special treat Amir and Sijavish were allowed to go, too.

We had not been there long when Sijavish's head dropped upon the shoulder of his nurse and she carried him home to bed. But Amir and I did not sleep. We turned and twisted, and wiggled and made noise and finally we were sent from the play to take a walk with the nurse of Amir. In the star-lighted darkness the wide-spreading land looked like a fearsome thing. I was used to the mountains behind Teheran. Now I looked about and saw nothing. Nothing. The melon fields were out of sight and all I saw was desert. Often I looked down at myself to see if my stomach were really swelling with the melon as I felt it was.

The next day Amir took me to see many people of the village. Everybody loved Sank so they were kind to us. Fahri and Fahti sat in the home receiving callers.

That afternoon I wanted to go to the bathhouse. Fahri and Fahti had been but they offered to send Sijavish's nurse with me. But I was grown up. I was grown enough to go traveling. I went alone. At the bathhouse, which looked very much like the one I was used to in Teheran, was a very thin dark woman who came to bathe me. "Lie down, dear," she said.

Lie down! I had never done that in the bathhouse in my life. I had always sat up while I was washed. "Lie down," she insisted, "so I can clean you nice." Finally I did.

I looked down at my body, tiny, firm mounds rising where not long before had been the bone cage of my ribs. It was the first time in my life I had felt naked.

On the last day of our visit I said, "I want to buy a gift for Mother and for Ali. Where is the city?"

Sank laughed. "Show her, Amir," he suggested.

Amir took me to the bazaar; one booth or two where there were tea and sugar and not much besides on sale. I was disappointed, but not for long. When I got back to Fahti's house one of their friends had left a gift for me—a rooster and a beautiful hen. The hen had feathers that gleamed like copper, but on closer notice were blue and green and brown, and each feather curled. She was a lovely creature. And the very first day she made for me a double-yolked egg!

When we left Fahti's house the rooster and hen, in a little cage home that one of the servants had made for them, went with us in the shining black rented car.

There was much grown-up talk that I did not understand. Only this, that Sank was leaving this village to go to a city in the north. For the first time I heard the word "industrial" used many times by both Sank and Ashbage.

It had been very hot all the time we had been in the village and we had all slept on pallets in the open court. Now as we rolled away through the melon fields the day seemed hotter than ever. We had traveled perhaps for two hours when the rumble of thunder came to us from the west; then there was the roar of thunder almost upon us and ribbons of red-blue light cut through the gray-black sky. And then it rained. The driver stopped the car because he could not see to go forward through the wall of water that reached from the sky to the earth.

This pouring of water did not last very long, I guess, but it seemed to the four of us waiting in the car that the time was very stretched. At last the driver started the car and pushed forward through the lessening downpour. We were stopped by a deep, wide river where there had been only a dry gully before.

"We had better return to the village," Ashbage said, and the driver turned the car around. In a short time we were faced by another new wide rolling river.

Now Fahri was crying. "What shall we do?" she kept crying, and I worried about my hen and her husband waiting in their narrow box.

The driver got out of the car. In a few minutes he came back. "There is a house on this island," he said. "The people in the home will take us in."

"No," said Fahri, but Ashbage said, "Of course. That's what we'll do."

Fahti had sent a great lunch with us in a package so we carried it into the home and shared it with the man and woman and twin children there. The woman made tea and we all drank to stop our shivering in the wet cotton clothes that stuck to our very cold damp bodies.

"We will stay for the night," Ashbage decided and he brought in the suitcases so we could dry our wet clothes at the fire of the home. When I had changed my clothes I slid down between the twin children in the home and went at once to sleep. Ashbage and Fahri sat all night by the fire. In the morning Fahri's beauty was spoiled by her tired red eyes and her tight face. "How could you, Najmeh? How could you lie down with those children? On that floor! They might have had lice! They might have had roaches."

I was very rested and happy. "We are all people. All alike, I think," I said.

Fahri looked long at me. "You are without a mind." With a very sarcastic voice she said, "I wish we were all as stupid as you are!" Then with a long, tired sigh, "And as rested."

Mother was glad to see us and to return Ali to Fahri, but

she was not specially glad to see my hen and rooster. She let me keep them in the court, though, and how I did keep them! The rooster I left pretty much to himself, he was an independent sort of creature, but the hen I played with constantly. Every day I washed her shining, curly feathers. One day I found her very stiff with her toes turned up. One of the servants buried her while Ali and I looked on; Ali, eyes round; I, weeping.

"She killed it with care," said the woman who came to our home for washing and ironing.

"Yes," Zarah agreed. But nobody objected to my crying for three days, and nobody urged me to eat until the three days of crying were over.

It seemed a very few days from the time that I entered the court of the school with my little girl friend until I took the final examinations and completed the six grades. I had now finished all of the education that my country furnishes free of charge. From this point on schools would be private and expensive. I felt that I must go on to school and my mother agreed. It is fortunate for me that my mother's father was a diplomat in Russia during the time that she was a child. In Czarist Russia she had seen Western ideas and Western ways and she could understand why I felt that I must go on to the high school.

There was a new modern high school not too far from our home in Teheran. Several girls from my class who belonged to the best families continued on through the ninth grade. At this age most girls stop school to marry.

Planning to go on to school was not at all unusual, but the summer after I had finished the sixth grade I did make a request that surprised every one. An American sewing machine company had opened a sewing school in Teheran. Women who bought a sewing machine might attend the school. I began to beg for a sewing machine. Three hundred dollars! That seemed an exorbitant price to my mother. Many things could be purchased with three hundred dollars; besides she had a good sewing machine in the house.

Mother's sewing machine, marked with the same big S that was on the new machines, was a long shuttle, treadle machine which had been part of her dowry and which was working more than twenty-five years later as well as it had on the day that it was carried through the streets by two perspiring servants to her first married home.

"I must go. I must!" I insisted.

"You are a child. A baby!" Mother said and Zarah agreed.

Suddenly it occurred to me that learning to sew would fit in with my growing dream of traveling. It was well that I was a child, a baby. If I could learn to sew now I could earn the money for traveling before I was seventy-five like the old woman in the story of The Match. I had decided some time before that I would rather make the trip by ocean liner and by train than on the back of a bird.

"Three hundred dollars," my mother wailed, but I saw a glance go between her and Zarah. Perhaps she was remembering the time when I cut out the doll dress with my teeth because she was afraid to give me scissors, my business of making dresses for other girls' dolls, my constant interest in sewing. Or maybe she was remembering how set I am on things when I know what is right for me.

Just the year before I had said to my mother, "I need a new dress."

"You can't have a new dress," Mother answered.

"Why not."

"Because."

"Is it that you don't have the money?"

"I have the money, but I will use it for flowers for the home."

"I must have a new dress."

Tried beyond endurance my mother snapped, "Be quiet!"

I went to my room. For two days I didn't eat or talk. Finally my mother came to me and said, "I'm sorry, Najmeh. You do need a new dress."

I was sorry, too, because my mother looked older and very unhappy, but I knew what was good for me and I did need the dress more than the home needed the flowers.

Now as Zarah and Mother traded a glance I wondered if they were remembering. Finally Mother said, "You may have the machine, Najmeh. You may go to the sewing school. But—"

I knew that in Mother's hesitant "but" there was a warning that I was not to take the sewing school too seriously. She did not want me to have a trade, a business. In two or three years I should marry, and then it might be useful to know how to sew.

How wonderful the sewing school was! There were six in the school. Two girls not quite so young as I, two women, and an instructor. The instructor was a Persian woman who had been away to study and she knew all about Western styles as well as about the sewing.

First we learned hand sewing, and I made some very beautiful curtains of net with appliquéd design. It was with a feeling of happiness that I discovered I shared a little at least in the aptitude of my people for design. After a time we began to use the machine. I had already learned to sew a straight seam on my mother's machine, but now I learned how to do all sorts of things with speed and ease.

A machine is almost more than a person, I thought. It can do so many things and so quickly. And, thinking of my mother's long-lasting machine, it seemed to me that machines well treated have almost an eternal life, too.

The first article I made on the machine was a dress for myself. Mother had purchased the cheapest muslin since she planned on my wasting the material, but the dress, made from a picture in a French fashion book, was lovely.

Sewing is simple in America. You select the style in a book, buy a paper pattern, read in English how to take every step from the cutting through to the finishing. In Persia, while there are patterns to be purchased, the instructions are in French or in English—usually in French—and most people can't read so the pattern has lost much of its value. In Persia we are more likely to look at a picture, take our own measurements, and cut without a pattern or with one of our own making. For the first dress I made in the sewing school, I made a basic pattern from an old dress which fitted me.

I was just ten, but as I sewed I planned that someday sewing would earn the money that would take me traveling. The dream was my own. I told it to no one. But when autumn came and it was time for the sewing school days to end and days at the high school to begin, I resolved to return to the sewing school the next summer, and the next, until I learned to be one of the best sewers in Persia.

I think now that during those happy days at school and in the sewing school I was completely selfish. Very seldom did I think of Zarah's words—"There is no one hungry in Persia tonight." But those words and their meaning were lying asleep deep in my heart. They were not really dead; only covered with dreams of traveling, with an expanding knowledge of the world, with the realization of growing powers and abilities and desires within myself.

## ⋆ 5 ⋆

# I KNOW HUNGER

M Y PEOPLE are a sad people. They can be merry, they can seem happy, but underneath the waves of gaiety there is the unfathomable deep of hopelessness, and helplessness and sorrow. Perhaps you would call it the understanding of reality, the racial knowledge that despite the goodness of God there is much that man must endure, much that he must triumph over. I think that this is the reason why religious observances in which weeping and wailing and suffering are a part are so important in our national worship. It is a custom in my country to gather in the cemeteries in Friday, our religious day, to mourn. I have seen the observance of Memorial Day in America. I have heard the bands, seen the parades, listened to the orators; I have felt the happy holiday mood of the people. In the cemeteries I have seen brightly dressed women arranging flowers on the graves of their friends and relatives. I have seen children skipping from one headstone to another. But nowhere have I heard the wail-like chant that is heard any Friday in our cemeteries.

Some people say that the crying and moaning is for show.

I think it is not; nor is all the weeping done for the dead. It is an opportunity to break through the quiet suffering calm of every day and for the time at least empty the heart of sorrow.

I think that the celebration of Moharram is for the same purpose though it is in reverence to Ali and Hussein and Hassan.

We who are Shiites believe that the only legitimate heir and successor of Mohammed is Ali, both by birth and by the will of the prophet. Of course the Sonni Moslems do not agree with us. They do not believe that the first three caliphs, Abu Bakr, Omar, and Othman, were really usurpers. That is why there are two branches of the Islamic faith.

Finally Ali became caliph, but his enemies were still busy and Ali was stabbed and his second son, Hussein, and all of his family were killed. Mohammed passed charism to Ali and Ali passed it on to his sons. Charism is a sort of divine grace, an infallibility, a sinlessness. This charism was passed down twelve times. Shiites believe that there were twelve Imams who like Ali were infallible and sinless and capable of interpreting divine will to the people. The last of the Imams did not die. He disappeared. When he comes again it will be the end of time for all of us. Other Imams are buried at holy shrines and there the people go to do them honor.

In our country there are little shrines, too, called Imamzadehs where one may pray if one cannot make a long trip to Mecca, Kerbela, Nejef, or Meshed.

Not too long ago the *Tazzieh*, passion play, was enacted the first ten days of Moharram. Moharram is not just a lunar month—rather it is a period of a month's duration set aside for religious observance just as many Christians set aside the period of time called Lent. During these first ten days the

*Tazzieh* was presented with such realism that everyone could
see and feel the martyr death of Ali and his house. The Shah
and his harem attended the play, always, as did everybody else
who was near enough to a city or a large village.

For each of the first nine days of the month of Moharram
a procession moved slowly down the street. Each man in the
procession wore a black robe and his back was bare. He carried
a lash or steel chain with which to beat himself. As the men
marched they gave themselves over to an ecstasy of sorrow,
beating their own backs until the blood ran from open welts.
On the tenth day the sword took the place of the lashes, and
white robes took the place of black. Now they cut themselves
with the swords; more and more excited they became until
they were even lashing at their hands and faces, the excitement
serving as sort of an anesthesia. Sometimes they fainted from
loss of blood, or from too intense ecstasy and were carried
away on litters.

Of course the women never joined in these processions. In
my country women are unworthy. In the old days black-
dressed women watched from the roof tops, adding to the
sound of wailing; marveling at those who lead the processions,
their flesh thrust through with pins and flesh hooks.

These processions used to be given in every city, in every
large village; but in 1935 Reza Shah made them illegal. First
the prohibition was against flagellantism. No longer could the
procession move slowly down the streets crying "Ya Ali, Ya
Hassan, Ya Hussein." Still the *Tazziehs* were enacted; then
they were forbidden. In the covered squares of the bazaars
men and women, separated, sat on carpets and listened to the
tragedy of the house of Ali recited by a mullah with enough
passion to set everybody to wailing and crying. Finally, these

public meetings were forbidden, too. But still a householder could fly a black flag and announce that in his home the passion of Ali would be ready. The black flag is called *Rosekhaneh.*

There is one celebration in which I did join when I was nine; that was the fast of Ramazon. During the month of Ramazon—Ramazon, like Moharram, is a period of a month's duration set aside for religious purposes, not just a regular month on our calendar—it is not right to eat during the hours of daylight. This month of fasting reminds Moslems that Mohammed fasted to purify his body and to teach his heart what the hunger the poor must endure really is. Strictly, one is supposed to eat just once a day, that is dinner, lunch, breakfast rolled into one meal, just after sunset.

In our home we followed Ramazon a little differently. I am sure that many families, especially with skinny children like me, did the same. About three hours before dawn we arose, and while it was still very dark we had breakfast. Ordinarily the breakfast was fruit, rice, tea, eggs, bread—a heavy breakfast.

After breakfast we sat together for an hour and I read the Koran to my mother. I do not know why I read the Koran rather than my mother, or one of my brothers. It was just natural for me to lead the family devotion. "Angel," Mother called me and I was happy in the name. After the reading of the Koran there was prayer and then we all went back to bed. It is a good idea to sleep as much as possible when one is fasting.

At mid-morning we rose and went to church. In the church we heard reading from the Koran, sermons from the mullah, and we prayed for ourselves and in unison. One must cry, too, for the service is supposed to be a service of mourning. These are the arranged items in the service. Not arranged, but certainly expected by anyone who knows my people, is the yak-yak of the women. There is so much to talk about when the only places for the meeting of women are in the churches and bathhouses.

After the services we went home, to sleep, if we could; if not, to look forward to the evening meal, making ourselves hungrier by conjuring up all manner of food in the mind until the memory of sight, and smell, and taste was almost too much to bear.

Afternoons, moping about the house, longing for food, I thought often of the hungry people of Persia; people to whom a fast came not just for one month out of the year but every day after every day.

At about sunset, preparations for dinner were begun. This was a poor time for a child to be under the feet of Ootah, but the food smelled so good! The cold foods—breads, cheese, fruit—were put on the table. I ran outside to look at the sky; the sun was still beaming over the roofs of the city. I went back into the dining room and gazed hungrily at the food.

Even as I stood there Ootah came in with a plate of desserts to place on the table. On it was a piece of chocolate. Chocolate!

Now I began to reason. (I was nine so I was old enough to figure things out for myself.) Why, I thought, do we eat before the sun is up and after it is down? The answer was easy. God must not see us eat. Is it not true that one sees only in the light; and since God has so many places to look at the same time He would need even more light than the rest of us?

Where could I go where God would not see me? Truly the

only sin is in being seen by God, not in eating, or we wouldn't
eat at all during the fast. I lifted the wide cover that hung
to the floor on each side of the table. Under the tent made
by the cloth and by the table there was real darkness. Quickly
I took the chocolate, secreted it in my two hands, and crawled
under the table. There, safe from the eyes of God, I ate it
slowly and thoughtfully. The candy was not made bitter
through a sense of my sin; it was the best chocolate I had
ever eaten.

Just at sunset a chant rose in the street, carried on the
voices of many men, that the time for eating is coming. But
before the eating there must be prayer. The prayer is to thank
God for the food. Then the eating that follows!

After dinner many families celebrate in their own homes. A
strange thing in Persia is that there are few clubs, few social
organizations as you know them in America. The center of
social life is the family. For larger parties the family relatives
are invited; for even larger, friends.

For some this celebration lasts a long time, probably until
the hour for the pre-dawn meal, with cards, and dancing and
drink; but for the faithful it is cut short so that the family can
again attend church and repeat the services of the morning.

Two days before the end of the month every woman assem-
bles a new wardrobe. The new clothes will go to church as
yours do on Easter Sunday. Some think that the brilliant
clothes on the women look strange in the old-world church,
but I like it. I am used to it.

In my country the minaret is the symbol for a man's soul.
Just as the minaret reaches toward heaven, so the individual
soul of man must reach alone toward God. Every man prays
for himself. So on this morning that is like your Easter every

man and every woman enters the church with a personal prayer to offer to God. What are these prayers? I do not know what the men are thinking. Probably, "Please, God, may we have rain?" Or, "Please, God, bring us peace." I do not know. I do know the prayers of the women. "Please, God, give me a husband before I fade and am no longer desirable," or maybe if one is a mother, "Please, God, help me to get a dowry together for my daughter."

For years on end women had no place in the churches and now when they attend they carry their woman nature with them.

Now everybody begins to look for the crescent moon which announces the close of the month of Ramazon. All the faithful except nursing mothers and children under nine have been hungry so long that they are looking forward to release more than they are concentrating on abstract sorrows.

At last comes the night of predestination.

In the church there is a solid roof of brightness from the light overhead. The faïence pillars glow with the light, the rich carpet on the floor is more radiant in color. We are kneeling on the floor in long lines, our faces turned toward Mecca or Medina. From the pulpit come the words of the preacher, but because of the shape of the church and the great dome of the ceiling it seems that his voice is everywhere. Tonight he talks very solemnly. He speaks often of God. Every time that he speaks the name of God we put our faces to the floor with a great sound. There is ecstasy in this experience. There is the losing of one's body in the expression of one's soul. I am carried away by the beauty. I look about me at the sensitive faces of the women. Never have I seen them so beautiful. Hunger has cleaned them down to the fine, beautiful bones.

The eyes look deep and enormous. I glance at my mother. Always I am told that I look like her. Seeing her now I am happy that I do. Although she is in her early forties her hair is as white as silver above the pale ivory of her face.

"God is the light," reads the mullah.

"God is the light," we repeat. And again we put our foreheads to the carpet with a great praying sound. My heart is about to burst with the pressure of the religious ecstasy.

Soon will come the crescent moon and Ramazon will be over for another year. During the month of Ramazon Teheran has been very quiet. Reza Shah had made it illegal to close the bazaars, but very few people are abroad in the day. But with the coming of the crescent moon the city will awaken to joy and celebration and feasting.

I was glad to be grown up enough to participate in the fast. I was no longer a baby. But I thought, even then, that Reza Shah must be right in demanding that the people should not spend the whole month in inactivity. It seemed to me that people could draw near to God, still working day by day. Perhaps I was too practical. Perhaps, even though I was a little child, the West had already begun to touch me with its influence and draw me away from the ancient ways. I searched my heart. I found that I loved God, that I honored God, that I realized that from God comes all that is good.

I thought again of the villages. Now that I had been hungry I understood Zarah's words. Sometime, I decided, I will find out why some people are always hungry and others are fat from feasting.

# • 6 •

# THE THREE-DAY WAR

W HAT is the matter, Mother? What is the matter?" I kept asking, looking with a sort of uncertain fear into my mother's face.

"Everything is all right, dear," she soothed me, but still she shook my hand from her skirt and went hurrying away to talk with a servant who at that time was doing our family marketing.

"What is the matter, Mosen?" I turned to my brother.

"War. That is what is the matter," he said half sullenly. "Fighting and killing."

I had seen fighting and killing in the American Western movies but in those no one that you admired or trusted was ever hurt. Fighting and killing were for wiping away wickedness. All this I explained to Mosen. "You are a baby," he said. "You are stupid. You have no head."

"I have, too, a head," I cried, trying to stop Mother to settle Mosen, but Mother spoke sharply to both of us.

I ran down the avenue to Fahri's home. "What is this war?" I asked Fahri as I stumbled over Ali playing in her courtyard

73

"Who knows?" asked Fahri. "But the British and Russians are bringing us war."

I felt as if I dreamed a nightmare. Everybody around me so uncertain and worried. I did not know that twenty years before, my country had promised Russia that in case Russia was threatened by a third power by way of Iran, Russian troops might enter Iran to remove such a threat.

I do not know whether or not Mother knew this, or Mosen. I am quite sure Fahri didn't. But all the grownups were reading the papers. The papers said that Russia had asked Reza Shah to imprison all of the Germans who had come to build the trans-Iranian railway, all those who had gone into business in Iran.

"Imprison." That was a word that I knew. In Persia many had been imprisoned by order of Reza Shah. One of the first things that I could remember were the raids that gathered in the rebellious young men and held them while Reza Shah overrode the religious feelings of the people to work his tremendous plan of modernization. Even the best friend of Reza Shah, Teymourtache, had been put in prison and had died by poison or strangling. A firm hand had brought Persia out of its ancient ways and that hand had often used the prison.

"Do we like the Germans?" I asked Ashbage. He with my mother and Fahri were sitting tensely in front of the radio.

"Would you please keep still?" Mother said very loudly for her. Then more softly, "We must listen to the radio, Najmeh. It tells of the war."

Mosen answered my question. "We don't like the British and the Russians. Besides, the Germans are winning. Already they are moving into Russia from the West."

"Why don't we like the British?"

"They are empire builders, that's why." And he tried to explain to me from his half knowledge about the British in India, about British holdings in Iran.

I remembered the very small splash of color on the school globe that was the British Isles. "Who is this that squeezes the people of the world in a closed hand?" I asked.

It was not a question to be answered. Mosen said, "But we'll show them!"

For twenty years Reza Shah had been building toward this time. He rejected the proposals of the Russians and the British. Persia was a sovereign state and for the Russians and British to send armed troops across the borders would be an unprovoked invasion.

I do not know why I remember these things. These snatches from the radio, these glimpses at the headlines. Perhaps it is because my mind was made acute by fear. For the first time since we had moved into our second home the house was filled with fear and tension.

The radio announced that again the Russians and British had written a note, this time demanding that Germans be expelled. Again Reza told these countries they must not interfere with Iran.

I thought that Reza was very brave and very right. I had seen, with everybody else in Teheran, the great military parades that took from morning until evening to pass along Galalieh, the street of the parade. The soldiers marched and the military equipment—guns, tanks, armored cars—passed slowly. It was not just the people that were impressed with these parades—it was the consulates of foreign powers as well. Everywhere in Teheran, every day in the year, there were soldiers. Everywhere. I did not know at that time that for

reasons of personal safety Reza Shah had most of the army
near Teheran, very little on the borders.

Then the family gave up everything but the sitting around
the radio. What next? Over the radio came the announce-
ments that Russia was moving in from the north. People had
said that the Russians would not spare troops to march into
Iran when the Germans were pushing across their Western
borders. Maybe that was why we were surprised and what
forces we had fell back.

Guests in our home said that in Azerbaijan there were those
who were ready to help the Russians. I do not know. From the
south the British began to move. For the first time in my home
there was talk of bombing. Where would we go? What would
we eat?

Mother sent the servants to buy what food could be had
in the market and others to prepare the cellar for living. Fahri
packed a suitcase which she took with her wherever she went.
In it she put soap, perfume, jewelry, delicate stockings. All
luxury. Even in the strain of war the family teased Fahri. But
she would go no place without the suitcase.

I remember the next few days as being days for the best
eating. As food was brought into the house and put away for
emergency much was prepared. And we ate all the time. All
the time biting into a fresh, juicy peach, or cutting a slice
from a succulent melon. It seemed it made waiting and fear-
ing easier to have a full stomach, a busy jaw.

"The Germans will save us," people soothed themselves.
And one guest in the home said, "If the Germans are coming
I'll be the first to put on flowers for Germany." We had not
heard at that time of the fanatical intolerance of the Germans.
We knew only the Germans who had been employed in Iran,
and we liked these men very much.

Came word on the radio that the British had blown our navy out of the Persian Gulf. Then, that Russia had actually bombed Tabriz. About Tabriz the people were really angry. They itched to fight hand to hand with Russians. Several thousand people had been killed in Tabriz. Not soldiers, but people had been killed. Teheran might be next.

Three days and Reza Shah gave the cease-fire order. The people were furious. Three days and the war was over. The family sat in the salon of my mother without words. Twenty years preparing for these three days. For this the boys from the villages had been brought into the army and released far from home so that they had become a horde of out-of-work tramps. For this taxes had been so high that the bank had posted a sign that it would no longer take the last samovar, the one rug of the poor in exchange for money. For this a railroad and truck roads had been built from the blood of the people so that foreign armies could cross and recross my country.

Everywhere there was a sick feeling. Even I realized that in spite of the grand showing of military force on parade, we had not even been able to fight. Twenty years had gone for less than nothing.

A week later Mosen came in breathless with news. "Three hundred cars have left the palace," he said.

"No!" said my mother.

"Three hundred at least," Mosen insisted. "And they had suitcases, too. The people did. I think Teheran is moving away."

Sometime later the radio announced, "Reza Shah Pahlavi has abdicated in favor of his son, Mohammed Shahpur."

"That's who was leaving the palace in three hundred cars. Did you see Reza Shah?" I cried.

Mother turned to me. "Would you like to keep quiet, please? I must hear the radio."

We knew, though the radio didn't say so, that Mohammed Shahpur had fled with the others. In four days he returned. With him was his wife and his mother, the old Queen. The young Queen, her five children, and Reza Shah's sisters did not return.

"What will the young Shah do?" Everybody was asking.

He soon answered. He gave the power back to the people. The Majlis, members of our parliament, who had nodded yes for Reza Shah, were now going to take charge of the government.

I heard talk of this, only half understanding what I heard. Mostly I heard the cry for bread.

"Wheat is going to Russia," we heard. "Rice is going to Russia." And then, "Our dates are rotting on the trees while we starve. Our enemies use the trains and the trucks and the roads for war transportation."

Now there was real hunger in Teheran. It was fortunate that my mother had laid in a supply, but still we must be careful. No one knew how long this cry would last. We must not be entirely without. If we went anywhere in Teheran we could not step without being jostled by the hungry beggars. We could not give to all. We soon would not be eating ourselves.

Every day there was less food. The first winter was not nearly as hungry as the next. Friends told us that at the Hotel Derbend, a very beautiful hotel in Shimran, they served only spinach and eggs and camel thorn. We must do something, but what?

"We ought to use camels," my mother said. "Camels. When I was a child—"

But in western Persia there are few camels. Reza Shah had ordered them off the roads because they slowed traffic. Near Meshed there were camels, going and coming with the food, but not near Teheran.

The radio told us that the British had brought in 93,000 tons of wheat. That Russia would maybe do the same. I do not know who saw that wheat.

In the spring came the American soldiers. "What is America doing here?" people asked. It is too bad that women are without political knowledge, without opinion. There is so much more fear where people are ignorant. "Why is America here?" everyone asked, and there was no answer.

We did not know that they had been sent in to operate the railroad and keep the trucks moving. We only knew that they had no business being there. We had fought a three-day war with Russia and Britain. We had had to let them in because we had lost that war. But with America we had never fought and now suddenly everywhere were American uniforms.

One day Ali and I went to a picture show, accompanied by my mother's driver. When we drew up near the theater two American soldiers grinned into the car. The driver's face went black with anger but he was helpless. He couldn't stop their grinning, their staring.

At that time we were angry with America. American soldiers had money and money and money to spend. They gave the hungry girls American sweets. They bought them dresses and trinkets. And they gave some of them babies and disease.

Six months after World War II was finished the Americans left. My country got over being angry. Among all the world nations it is America that Iran, in normal times, trusts most, I think. It is my belief that if Britain had transferred her holdings in the Anglo-Iranian oil to American companies the people would not have demanded and insisted on the nationalization of the Iranian oil.

It is strange how one gets used to even very bad things. I was to be almost fourteen before the Americans and British left my country. Older than that before the Russians, leaving military supplies in the hands of disloyal Persians, and refusing to pay for the damaged roads and railways, finally withdrew.

But soon life went on much as usual. Reza Shah was in Johannesburg and the new King sat on an almost useless throne.

## • 7 •

# TIME FOR SUITORS

THE other day in an American history class I memorized these words from the American Declaration of Independence: "We hold these truths to be self-evident, that all men are created equal, that they are endowed by their Creator with certain inalienable Rights, that among these are Life, Liberty and the pursuit of Happiness."

And I thought these words are more true in Persia than they are in America if the word men really means men. In my country there is now no race discrimination; there is no creed discrimination—Parsees (Zoroastrians), Nestorians (Christians), and Moslems (Mohammedans) all have equal rights and privileges; there is no color line, no caste as in India.

There is one half of humanity in my country, however, that has no right to vote, no right to hold office, that until eighteen years ago was considered unworthy even to associate with men outside the home.

Women in Persia, as in most other Islamic countries, are a race apart, an inferior, limited race.

Reza Shah tried hard to change this, but such things—attitudes—cannot be changed by law. He made it against the law to wear the veil, even against the law to drive a woman who wore a veil anywhere in my country.

A clever woman can say much with a veil. She can make it alluring and romantic. But there is something important and hard for women of the West to understand in this practice of keeping the face always covered. The veil excludes women from the world of men; it is an acknowledgment that she is different, of less value.

When Mohammed was living he saw men burying female infants alive in the sand. He felt that it was a great wickedness. Yet he did not blame men for preferring sons:

They ascribe daughters unto God! far be it from Him! but unto themselves sons, the sex they desire.

And when any of them is told the news of the birth of a female, his face becometh black (he is ashamed) and he is deeply afflicted.

He hideth himself from the people, because of the ill tidings which have been told him; considering within himself whether he shall keep it with disgrace, or whether he shall bury it in the dust. Do they not make an ill judgment?

Unto those who believe not in the next life, the similitude of evil ought to be applied, and unto God the most sublime similitude, for He is Mighty and Wise.

These words are from the Koran, Sura 16:57. Also from the Koran are the words: "And when the female infant who hath been buried alive shall be asked for what crime she was put to death. . . . Then every soul shall know what it hath wrought." Sura 81:1.

He was far in advance of the thinking of his time; that is why he confined polygamy to four wives who could be kept well and treated kindly. But because the regulations he made for women at that time became a closed law in Persia and other Islamic countries, women didn't gain slowly a place in the world as women in the West did.

The veil has been abolished by law, but I have seen women in the villages take the veil worn over the head between the teeth so as to cover the face if a stranger approaches. Very recently a woman is allowed to work outside of her home in a factory or office or shop, but still a woman of high class is supposed to be a doll—a very pretty, charming, obedient, alluring doll.

The Bath House.

Some new rich who have taken on Western ways very rapidly allow their women to meet in public places and to drink tea and other things, to play cards, to shop in the Westernized stores. But in the old conservative families men will not allow their wives and daughters such liberties. Necessary shopping is done mostly by servants or by women and girls attended by servants.

For many years the only place where it was proper for women and girls to go was to church or to the bath.

It is very nice to have a bathtub in each home. Very convenient. More and more families who are building modern

European-type homes in the new sections of our old cities
are having this luxury. There are, too, modern public bathhouses where you can go and have a tight little cubicle con-
taining a tub, a bowl, maybe a shower, locked away from the
rest of the world.

Me, I like the ancient ways. Much better than a newspaper,
much better than a weekly magazine, much better than a
bridge party, even better than the modern beauty salon, is the
ancient bathhouse of my country. It is the place for giving
and receiving all news. It is the place for all female yak-yak
and much else besides. There is a bathhouse in each village
and in the cities like Teheran there are many and one can
choose according to the financial and social standing of the
family.

The bathhouse that I like best has not been changed in
the memory of man. It is built of brick—as all of these houses
are. The door is level with the avenue, but once you step over
the threshold you must descend eight or ten steps to reach
the floor level. A very thin woman sits on a sort of stool behind
a high table, looks at you keenly to make certain that you are
a Moslem and of the right class to be bathing at her establishment, takes your money, and motions to a seat against the
wall.

No foreign people enter these ancient baths. They might
not be "clean." All around the large room with its brick
walls painted in steam-softened colors, perhaps fifteen by
twenty-five feet, there is a brick ledge for sitting and for
holding the bath case you have brought. In the center of the
room is a square pool of cold water. This is not for bathing.
There is a short passageway that leads from this room to the
real bath, as you say, "Turkish bath." Here the air is com-

forting with steam. All around the room, even larger than the other, is a very low brick ledge for sitting. We have undressed in the other room and now each woman sits upon a brightly lacquered tray to be certain that she is sitting on a clean place. Now will come the attendants of the bath to wait on us. There are bright copper bowls on the floor in front of each woman. These the attendants keep filled with hot water from the large pool at the end of the room.

I have a special attendant, more thin even than The Match, for whom I wait because I like the way she does. While she rubs over the body with her hand encased in a very soft-knitted bath mitten, someone else will be washing the hair; applying the henna. Henna is a custom in my country. It is not used for color but to make the hair strong. We are all women and there is no feeling of nakedness as we purr in the luxury of sweet-scented soapsuds, warm water, and gently massaging hands. There is much gaiety, much laughter. The best of food is sent from the homes, for this is an activity that will take several hours, and hot tea is served with the fruit and bread and other delicacies.

What do we talk about? Women things of course. Food, and children, and clothes, and husbands. Politics, too, because now that women are attending higher schools, even doing some work in the world of man, they are better informed about the world. Many women will quote their husbands on all important matters; men are still the head of the house and most often do the thinking for the women and hand down ideas as if their judgment were infallible.

But often when the young girls are at the bath the talk is of the girls themselves. This girl has a musical laugh, this one hair which curls even in the steam, this one a fresh sweet skin.

The women are constantly on the watch for suitable brides for their kinsmen; their brothers, their cousins, their sons.

From behind her copper washing bowl a dark thin woman with a straight-boned face half covers her mouth as her eyes travel over the body of a twelve-year-old russet-haired child. She whispers to her neighbor, "Who is that child?" The neighbor looks and shakes her head. With a gesture of the finger the woman calls the girl's bath attendant to her. "Who is that child? Of what family?"

Now the bath attendant glows with enthusiasm. She tells all she knows about the girl, information she has been procuring over a long period of time for just such an opportunity. This girl, she says, comes from the most ancient and honorable family in Teheran. She is kin to the royal family. There would be no Senate if her kinsmen did not sit in the law-making body. The family has wealth. The girl arrives at the bath in a great Cadillac with two uniformed servants. The girl is unspoiled by all this family importance, all this wealth. She is simple and sweet. Her hair is of fine texture and she hasn't a tooth missing. And her skin! Like pear blossoms to the touch.

Much of the account will be exaggerated but the woman who is asking can separate the truth from the fiction. She knows that if anything comes of a visit to the home of the girl in behalf of her son the bath attendant will expect from her a large tip.

There will be other remuneration to the woman, too. Two days before the wedding the girl will invite to the bathhouse twenty or thirty friends to spend the day in cleansing. Outside the place an orchestra will play beautiful or lively music, and for this function there will be a feast from the home of the bride. The attendant will share in the feast. There will be a gift to the woman who washes the bride of a fine new dress.

When the attendant answers a beckoning finger she must tell all the good, conceal the not-so-good, and add as much as is credible to the story, for she is playing for great winnings.

In the city bathhouse and in the bathhouse of the village, the conversation is the same. Always in the minds of the women there is a lively interest in the young girls. For the women are the suitors of Persia. When a young girl leaves her tray to go into the hot pool or to dip screaming into the adjacent cold pool, many eyes will follow her. The girl does not mind. She knows that the place that woman must occupy in her country is at best beloved doll to her husband and respected mother to her children. She is flattered at the admiring glances, and smiles inside herself at the tall tale that she is sure the bath attendant is telling.

The other day I wrote a letter to a girl friend in Persia and I told her that I still like best the Persian way of choosing a wife for a man. Women can see reality, real virtues, important things. Not for them will a pretty face cover a lot of evil temper and unclean thoughts.

The wife of a very exceptional American man once asked me, "What are you going to do when you finish school here?"

She is an intelligent woman, much interested in what is happening all over the world so I began to tell her about my plans. In a moment I realized that she had asked the question to make conversation so I brought my remarks to a fast finish.

"You don't want to do that," she said. "Why don't you catch an American husband?"

"Catch?" I said. "Catch?"

"Yes, I caught mine. He did not think of marrying me at first so I told him I wanted to marry him and he agreed."

I know that she is joking but still I don't like the American word "catch." At college I do not like the way American girls display themselves for the men. I suppose that I am truly ancient in my ideas about marriage.

I have watched the courtship of my two brothers with my mother doing the courting. Both of my brothers married friends of our family. Much of the regular procedure was eliminated. My mother had known the girls since they were little children so she did not have to set an inquiry around in the bathhouse. But there was other procedure she did follow.

It is the custom for the mother, with as many female relatives as care to make the call, to send a servant ahead to announce that she is making a call, object matrimony for her son. She goes into the house. The call is a polite one, but all eyes are open. The girl knows the eyes are upon her and she feels her knees knocking together, her smile made of cardboard on her face, her hands trembling. For this call she has prepared herself without make-up. Make-up might hide a blemish which the mother must see if she is not to be deceived. If her hair is straight it is combed straight, not "set" in handmade waves. My curly hair was born with me so I do not need to wear my hair straight for the suitors.

I have heard that some suitors rub the girl's hair between their fingers, even examine the teeth for strength and whiteness and wholeness. Most suitors, I think, can see these things without such an examination.

At the end of the ordeal the girl pours tea and shows her knowledge of grace and etiquette. If she is a musician she may sing or play a musical instrument, or if she is a dancer she may dance one of the traditional dances of my country.

Oh, the trying hour when the teapot feels as if it must jump from the hand; when the tea cup tries of itself to bounce upon the carpet!

Once outside the house there is much talking between the female suitors. "I saw—" says one. "You did!" The other rolls the eyes in disbelief. "Well, the thing I noticed was—" There is nothing left undiscussed.

If the suitors are pleased with the girl, with her accomplishments, with the wealth and position of her family, next time, very soon, the prospective groom will visit, too. The man will be older than the girl, maybe five years or so. Or maybe he will be a middle-aged or even an old man looking for a wife to take the place of one lost by death or to add to his harem.

Westerners are always interested in the harems of Islamic countries. Now they are not like the harem of King Solomon, nor like those in the *Arabian Nights* stories. A man is allowed by Koranic law to have four wives if he can provide for them and will be just to all of them; but few can afford to keep more than one wife and her family. And to be "just" to four at once? That would be a great challenge.

So most older men looking for a wife are those who have lost a wife through death. In America I heard of a widow in her middle sixties who had recently married a man of her age. I was surprised. A girl of fewer years than twenty would have been the choice of such a man in my country.

Reza Shah made a law forbidding child marriages. The girl, according to law, must be sixteen. But still many girls marry at eleven, twelve, thirteen. We have what we call in Farsi the *pishkesh* which stems from the statement that it is lawful for man to take what comes to him in line with his public office, Money changes hands and the young girl marries. In your country you call it the bribe but in mine it is an ancient and honorable custom.

The first suitor came to my house when I was eleven or twelve. I was at home alone, barefooted, watering can in one hand and a hard chewy cookie in the other. When I saw a carriage stop in front of my home I dropped the watering can in the court and hurried into the house in full view of the delegation of ladies who were alighting with the help of a footman.

We do not have bells, but knockers on our door. "Knock, knock, knock."

I pushed back the curtain from the small peephole in the door. "What do you want?" I asked, chewing on the cookie.

"We want to see the young girl of the house," the foremost woman said in a very sweet voice.

"I am the girl," I said, still chewing and not opening the door.

"Open the door, dearie," she coaxed. "You seem like a nice child."

Suddenly the awful thought struck me that I was grown up—that these women were suitors! "I'm not ready—for that!" I cried, dropping the curtain and retreating to the back of the house. "Go to another home, please. It is not time for me!"

The summer that I was fourteen an older cousin, Efaht, was visiting me and we were bored. We spent almost a day in the bathhouse but there was no diversion for the evening. We had heard a certain girl whom we didn't know discussed in the bathhouse. "Her mother," my bath attendant had told me, "is very eager to marry her daughter off. We've done all we can for her, but something goes amiss."

"There must be something wrong with such a girl," my cousin's attendant said.

Thinking about this conversation, later, gave us a project to see us over a dull evening.

We sent a servant to announce to this woman that suitors would call. When he returned the two of us dressed carefully, called my mother's chauffeur to take us in the car, and went to pay the call.

From somewhere within the house the mother must have seen the large car drive up. We were treated with the greatest respect. That poor girl! She served us fruit and tea and cake— everything of the best. She sang for us. She answered questions as did her mother. The mother told of the girl's dowry, praised her virtues, declared she had no shortcomings. Finally we withdrew. It was like leaving a bazaar where one has begun to bargain for goods he decides he does not want. The mother was reluctant to have us leave without a promise to return. She followed us to the door, still with praise of her daughter.

After Efaht and I got in the car the two of us laughed and giggled. Perhaps we enjoyed the whole thing because we were both reluctant to see suitors and were being subjected more and more often to such calls. We should have taken pity on the poor, white, shaking, eager girl. But we were too young to know pity.

I did not want to see suitors, but sometimes my mother consented to such calls, and I acted as gracious and grown up as I could. One day my sister Fahri called me and said, "Najmeh, I have special guests coming to my home. Will you come over and help me?"

Of course, I would be glad to.

"Come soon," she suggested. "And wear one of your nicest dresses. These are really important guests."

I hurried over and helped arrange the fruits and cakes and other things on the table. I worked with the flowers. When the guests came I was very, very gay. Sometimes I am like that, as if I can slip into a second personality, and tease and joke and send back bright words for bright words. Never did I spend a more pleasant evening.

After the guests had gone Fahri looked at me from under lowered lids as if she were ashamed of something. "Those were suitors," she said. "They wanted to meet you."

"You did this to me!" I cried, arranging my hands to fit around her neck. "To me!"

Now her blue eyes were wide open, laughing with a white light shining through her face. I laughed, too. No danger about those suitors returning!

But the next day they came back. They were pleased with the girl. She was so gay, so unself-conscious!

I decided not to marry. At least not for a long, long time. But it would be exciting to be betrothed. I was almost envious of my friends who were happily preparing for marriage. Wives are not purchased in Persia as some people believe. Nevertheless, a wife from the highest class is worth at least five thousand dollars in gifts.

After the call by the female relatives, after the boy (or man) has visited the home and has said that he is satisfied, then the parents of both the boy and girl get together to talk about the dowry of the girl, the gifts of the boy, the wedding, the ceremony, other matters.

The first gift of the groom's parents to the bride will be,

most likely, a diamond ring. If the parents can afford it, the stone will be enormous. It reflects the position of the family. After this will come the handwritten, beautifully illuminated copy of the Koran. This too is a very expensive gift. Later there will be such gifts as silver candlesticks done with the care and creative precision of the Persian artisan, silver mirror, lacquered chests—the gifts are reflections of the artistic culture of Persia.

For two or three months, maybe even for a year the bride will remain in the home of her mother getting her dowry arranged. In my country this is a happy time in the girl's life and in the mother's too, when the two work together for the life-long happiness of the girl.

As I grew older there were many suitors coming to my home. This does not mean that I was the most attractive girl in Teheran. Ordinarily suitors visit many girls before they make a choice. Sometimes, nowadays, the men, themselves, select a girl and ask their female relatives to make the first call. Of the many who called at my home there were several who wanted to call again. But I was not satisfied. Ordinarily the girl is not asked if she is satisfied. It is her business to satisfy! But my family understood me. My mother would have liked to have me marry well as Fahti and Fahri did, but she knew that a man who would make an excellent husband for ninety per cent of Persian girls would not be happy with me. I must have something more than a good man, a kind man, a man of good family, and position and means. I must have a husband who can read my heart if I open it to him. Who understands what I must do because I am I.

One holiday Amir came to our home in Teheran. We gave a party for him and invited all of the family in Teheran. One of my mother's distant kinsmen, a young man named Mohammed, came to the party. He and Amir made friends at once. After that whenever Amir was in Teheran Mohammed was likely to be with him. There was a friendly feeling between the three of us. Mohammed was good, clean, very intelligent. Perhaps if he had sent a suitor—

But no. I was not yet ready. I had many dreams, many wishes still unfulfilled. When I went to church I prayed, "God let me be just myself, just Najmeh, until I have done the things that I must do."

# · 8 ·

# THE ADVANCED SCHOOL

WHEN I was in high school something strange happened to me. I had been very quiet, very good, very obedient, very quick to learn. I had had a tender heart. But, suddenly I was gay, laughing, silly. Maybe I had lost my sensitivity. I do not know. It was a wonderful thing to be living; to walk down the street with my arm around my friend, Naheet.

We were going to the school which we girls called the Bastille. Though the school work was more difficult and the teachers even more stern, I was happy. The Bastille—we named our school for the famous French prison after reading about the French Revolution—was of course a girls' school. Many of the teachers were hard, unlovely women. In America you have a word to describe them—frustrated. In my country they were examples of what happens to the natural softness of women when they do not marry. To us they were cranky, mean, terrible.

Just two streets from our school there was a boys' school. That is why the teachers kept watch over us with both eyes. Even the school schedule was arranged to make the watching easy. If the school sessions began at the same time and ended at the same time in the afternoon, the boys and girls might be friendly. They might even speak to each other. If the boys were dismissed first, they would wait around for the girls. So the girls were excused early.

It was strange how long it took Naheet and me to walk a very little way—say two blocks—down the avenue. We were surprised to have just passed the boys' school when it was dismissed for the day. We never spoke to the boys, but we were learning the language of tossing the head until the curls jumped, of looking with eyes almost covered with shyly lowered lids. Sometimes a brave boy seized a book from us and escaped. We were flattered! We knew we were beautiful and full of charm. Sometimes the younger boys walked on their hands or turned handsprings so that we would notice them. We did.

This never talking together, the boys never discovering that girls are just people and the girls never discovering that boys are just people, is very bad, I think. It is one of the worst things in my country. The care that is taken to keep boys and girls separated makes us think always of sex. People grow hungry for forbidden food even when they are very young.

Already we had read about moonlight on the Seine and of how lovers walk hand in hand. I dreamed that someday it would be moonlight on the Seine for me. Many years later when I did see the Seine by moonlight—how can I tell you? Many men and girls were sitting on the sidewalks, kissing, caressing. I do not have correct words for all the things they were doing. I had read of these things. I had seen them in pictures. But when I saw them with my eyes, my legs softened and would not hold me and I felt sick.

The segregation of sexes in Persia is a bad thing, I think, yet never is it necessary to put the pot on such a hot fire that it must boil over!

I remember one teacher who was especially unlovely. I did not think then, but I do now, that she was especially hungry to be young and to be desired. One day I had my brown hair tied with two blue bows, one behind each ear holding a clump of curls. Our uniforms were not made alike but they were an ugly lifeless color of gray. I had one of mine made with a tiny red piping around the collar and pockets, the other trimmed with a piping of clean, clear blue. The bows on my hair matched this little piping and made the uniform look almost pretty.

"Why do you wear these ribbons?" she asked me.

"I want to be pretty," I said.

She pulled the ribbons from my hair. "They are wicked. They are for the purpose of decoration and decoration of women is for the purpose of bringing sin to the mind of boys."

I was angry and hurt. I knew the words of the Koran as well as she did: "And speak unto the believing women, that they refrain their eyes and preserve their modesty, and display not their ornaments. . . ." I was only a girl. I would never be anything more than a woman. I was angry that I was a woman, but that was one thing I could not change. At least I should be allowed blue bows in my hair.

It seems to me that since I have been in America I have discovered that everything that seemed like sin to the teachers in the advanced school in Persia is pleasure to young people in America. And I think in America boys and girls may make some little mistakes together, little by little, but they will not make the big mistake that can come to one who has had a growing hunger for a long time and suddenly must satisfy it.

Our literature teacher was a man who did not feel exactly at home with a room full of girls. He was supposed to be our Farsi teacher—Farsi is the pure Aryan language of my ancestors—but this he could not be. In Persia there are many, many dialects spoken. In the old days—even forty, fifty years ago—there was no easy going and coming across my country. Each district spoke its own language. Near the Turkish border the language was more Turkish than Farsi. And so it was where our country touched another, the Farsi was mixed with another tongue. This teacher was from Shiraz and he spoke with a very strong accent.

We girls laughed at his accent but he thought we were laughing at his little jokes. Because he was nervous with us, he lectured in a very grand manner. He had a way of snuffling which sounded almost like a snore. "Lend him your handkerchief so that he may blow his nose in the other direction," Naheet whispered to me, and we were off in a whirl of laughter.

In the front of the room was a large map. One day before the teacher entered, Naheet and I got behind this map instead of taking our seats. The girls were laughing and laughing.

"What is this?" he asked, but there was no answer. After a time he decided to use the map. He moved it and we jumped and ran to our seats. "Who is this? Who is this?" All the girls were laughing and looking at us so he looked at us, too. He made us each stand in a corner of the room with one foot and one arm raised. When he tried to go on with the class, one of us would make a dance movement that meant something to the other girls and they would laugh again.

My poor teacher.

Two years later the people of Shiraz saved him from the school and the silly girls by electing him to the Senate. Later

I met him again. His manners were perfect, his Farsi was much purer, he was a nice man. He must have been very miserable, really, in the Bastille.

Naheet and I were making the very best grades but we did not feel we were learning. About a mile from my home—an easy walk—there was a school of design. I decided that I wanted to go to school in this place and Naheet liked the idea, too. I had been sewing summers in the Singer School and had been made an assistant there. I knew that I wanted to learn design.

I had finished three years of the advanced school in two years and the teachers there wanted me to continue, but I had made up my mind. The next year I enrolled at the school for design.

There were many girls at this school, maybe two hundred, but I did not come too close to every girl, only to those in my own class. There were many teachers, coming to teach us special things. I remember the teacher who taught "The coat." He was French and spoke only in French. We did not understand the French, and he did not understand the Farsi so his lecture was not a real benefit to us.

The head of the school was a very beautiful, very big woman with perfect manners. She was not a person to love. She was withdrawn from us, and cold. She ran her school very well and though the girls whispered about her special favorites, we were all happy. In fashion art we were attentive and quiet, watching the way lines should be drawn and memorizing relative proportions. In pattern-making we were attentive, too, because we realized it was important.

But in the sewing class! Here we sang and talked and were happy.

Winter came and the big schoolroom where we sewed was

always cold. We would sit at the long tables, our feet drawn up under us, and complain that the fire had not been lighted in time to make us warm.

One morning, after we had complained many times, we came into the room and there was no fire. We all began to talk about it and someone suggested that we might burn the mannequin that we used for the fitting of dresses. It was wood. At first, no, but later when no one came to warm us, yes. Naheet and Mohannah and I took the mannequin to pieces and put it in the fireplace to burn.

When the janitress came to make the fire she saw the mannequin just beginning to curl and blacken in the heat. "The Lady will hear this," she said and hurried away, her big flat-soled shoes flapping on the bare floor.

Burning the mannequin had seemed very funny but now it did not seem such a good idea. The three of us went out of the sewing room, through the fitting room and into the washroom. Here there was one pane missing from a small window. Naheet, who was tiny, went through the opening very easily. I, who was a little bigger, pushed in head first and with just a little wriggling got through. But Mohannah! She was unlucky. Her head and body down to her waist was through the window, but her hips would not go through. The Lady came into the washroom and taking her by the leg pulled her back. We did not know this at the time. We were in the court hidden by the brown, leafless shrubs.

We did not know how to get out of the court. A man sat at the gate letting people through only if they showed the right paper, and Naheet and I had no paper. There was a little stream running in a tiled stream bed from the outside of the court into the center pool. To let the stream pass through the wall, a little half circle opening had been made when the wall was built. Through this little opening we squeezed and went home.

Mohannah did not tell the Lady that we had done these things. She told us the next day that The Lady had promised her a failure in her work.

All morning I sat sewing on the skirt I was making. Finally I went to the office of The Lady. "Twenty girls burned the mannequin," I said.

She would not listen. I, knowing that she would not listen, said, "Give me F. I burned the mannequin."

But she did not give me F. With an F, I would not return again to the school. When my examination dress was completed in the spring—white with delicate bindings of red, worn with red slippers, red gloves, a red bag—the school gave me A. Still I did not want to go back to the design school the next year. I had found during the winter that I missed books. I must live closer to books. There was much knowledge still for me to gain.

On a street we call Sadii there was a wonderful book store. Whenever my mother gave me money for stockings, for perfume, for little luxuries, I went to this store.

"What is the best in the books today?" I would ask the man in the book-lined room. He came to know me and to know my taste in books. It was easy for him to put into his cashbox the money that was given me for my own spending.

It was this way that I met Maeterlinck.

"Today we have something by Maeterlinck." He took two books into his hand. "I do not know if you will be interested. It is not *The Golden Dream*."

*The Blue Bird* is, in Persian, called *The Golden Dream*. I had seen the very beautiful picture with Shirley Temple, I think, and would have enjoyed that book. "What is it you have?" I asked.

"This, I have, is *The Life of the Bee*. And this, I have, *The Life of the Ant*."

"Are they of interest to you?" I asked. In my country we do not always say, "Is it *new*?" as some readers do in America.

The man put down *The Life of the Bee* and stood caressing the smooth white cover of *The Life of the Ant*. "I have never been more interested in a book," he said. "Maeterlinck truly reveals the mystery which lies just out of sight, beneath the surface of ordinary life."

"Is it difficult?" I asked.

"Difficult? H-m-m." The man pursed his lips. "In words it is not difficult, very very simple, in fact. In symbols it is not difficult. But in meaning! It may be too strong for you."

I bought *The Life of the Ant*. Later I bought *The Life of the Bee*. Still later I bought what is called in English, I think, *The Double Garden*, but which in Persian had a very different name. These I read and enjoyed very much. Three years later I read them and understood them. The simple words were intended to reach the mature mind.

I do not know how many Americans read Maeterlinck nowadays, but to me he is one of the greatest. Probably because his mind, like the Persian mind, turned to symbols for full expression. But perhaps because much of his philosophy sounds so true when it is tested by even simple experience.

"Experience still shows that we risk less by keeping our eyes before us than by keeping them behind us, less by looking too high than by not looking high enough. All that we have obtained so far has been announced and, so to speak, called forth by those who were accused of looking too high."

Another quotation which came to my mind more and more frequently is, "The harmonious use of liberty is acquired only by a long misuse of its benefits."

It was the summer after I attended design school that I again had the opportunity for traveling. Fahti, who now lived in the north, had written inviting Fahri and Ashbage and me to come to her for a ten-day visit. I was wild with excitement and so was my nephew, Ali, until he discovered that he was not to go. He was a big boy, then, ten years old, and he thought it was an insult to be left with Grandmother. He protested that Sijavish and Amir would want him to come; but this was to be a vacation for Fahri and she firmly said no.

In my country where the mothers are so very young they are very happy with their children, playing and singing and being young, too, but sometimes children make them nervous and tired. Fahri didn't want to be bothered with Ali on this trip. I was glad that I was fully grown so that I would be no bother at all.

This time, joy and joy, we were going by train. It was no longer a treat to go by automobile as our family now had a car and the driver brought it any time Mother called. But train travel—that was something different.

Ashbage and Fahri had much to say to each other. I watched her very beautiful face under the wide hat. She looked like a young girl on a holiday and Ashbage seemed to be a very new husband, he was so attentive and kind with her. I did not care if they talked only with each other. I wanted to see the new country.

We were traveling north through the hills, and away from the desert. The city that Fahti now lived in was on the Caspian Sea far from the desert that stretches away from Teheran. I will never forget the very green green of the Caspian country. I had been accustomed to a land of light rainfall. Here the rainfall is heavy and no plant is thirsty. After we had passed through the mountains we had been going down and down, too, and the air seemed to change.

Fahti with her chauffeur met us, and Fahti and Fahri kissed each other and laughed and looked into each other's face. I thought again that I should have had a sister of an age near to me, so that I would have the happiness of Fahri and Fahti. In a moment Fahti saw me standing off by myself. She put an arm around me. "Amir cannot wait for your coming," she said. It was as if Amir and Sijavish and I were of one family, my two sisters of another.

Fahri's eyes were shining when she saw Fahti's home. Sank was the chief official in this city and his residence was furnished by the government. It was very big for the entertaining of government guests and the furnishings were of the richest and best. Fahti, very small, very slim, did not seem to me big enough to run this place. But there were many servants who obeyed her requests.

We washed and said our devotions, then there was lunch. All the time Amir was saying, "When are we going, Mama?" and Sijavish was coaxing, too. Fahti threw her palms up with impatience. "There are no surprises in this home," she said. "We are going to the beach after lunch."

After we again washed and said our devotions, we got in the car to go to the beach. Ashbage had disappeared. He was probably somewhere with Sank. Cars in Persia are always driven by special drivers. People wealthy enough to own auto-mobiles can afford drivers. Those too poor to afford drivers cannot buy cars.

The driver got out of the car and set up a great striped umbrella for Fahti. He put many pillows under the umbrella. Fahti and Fahri sat under the umbrella; but I was at once in the water. It was cool and pleasant and clean. Amir got a large ball from the car. We threw it from one to the other until Sijavish grew so angry that he screamed and Fahti spoke for him.

"Are you without a head?" she asked me. "You will burn. I cannot understand why you want to be in the sun and water."

"She is a little girl," Fahri said, teasing me with her smile. But I did not mind. I was a little girl. I did not care for parties. I did not enjoy the formal things. I loved to play. The exercise, I think, was good for me.

"You should see the moon on the sea," Fahti said, but we did not wait to see it. That night Fahri and Ashbage and Sank and Fahti were invited to some formal reception.

The next day Fahti had an open house for us. Many of her friends were calling, just as they did in the village, to meet Fahti's sisters. She was a wonderful person, so happy that Fahri had great beauty. Not at all jealous of the heavy golden hair, the blue-green eyes, the milklike skin.

One day Sank took us to see the manufacturing in the town. It is here that the most beautiful of the pure silk is made. I watched the women and children at the loom. I wondered if they were like the village people. If there were bread in their homes. When I asked Fahti this, she answered, "No, I should say not. These people eat rice. This is rice country."

"How much do they earn?" I persisted.

"Sank will tell you. He knows all such things."

But somehow we were so busy I forgot to ask Sank.

That evening Fahti scolded a servant for some mistake. The girl was very hurt, very excited. "I'll kill myself. I'll eat bread," she cried.

Fahti comforted her before she turned to me. "That is what I told you. Many of these people think that bread is poison, only rice is food."

Another day my sisters and Amir and I went in the car to another town, Barbarsah. It was a show place of beautiful flowers, the most beautiful I have seen in the world. Of green, deep green, shrubs and trees, of many singing birds. When the world is so beautiful in the north I wonder why people live in the south.

Another day we all went shopping in the ancient bazaars. These were much like those of Teheran, only the displays of Persian costume were different, since the native dress changes with each province. Fahti laughed when Fahri and I spent half a morning selecting a dress for me, but since I had been to the school of design I was very interested. The foundation of the costume was a pair of ankle-length red pantaloons worn with a long-sleeved white blouse. Over the blouse was worn a hip length jacket of the red, sleeveless, and open several inches in the front. Over the pantaloons, a two-tiered white skirt, very full and above the knee in length. There was a white veil, rather coarse and heavy, to be worn over the head and pinned under the chin, and for the top of the head there was a little red felt brimless hat.

A woman has to be beautiful to look well in such a costume; but the women of Chalus are beautiful. The next day Fahri took pictures of me in the costume standing against a wall and holding a large bouquet of flowers like the Chalus women carry on special occasions.

When the ten-day vacation was over, Fahti and her driver took us to the train. Amir and Sijavish went, too. They waved and waved to us until we could no longer see them. I wished that these boys lived in Teheran. It had been such a pleasure to be with them. They were both good students. Amir told me his secret that someday he would go to England to school.

"How would you like to change places with Fahti?" Ashbage teased Fahri.

"I like Chalus," she said, "but that home of hers is like a hotel!"

The next fall I returned to the advanced school. Now, almost like a mysterious thing, I was no longer a very silly girl. I had my feeling back. I was again sensitive. I thought of the foolish girl hiding behind a map and I was ashamed. Now I was mature enough to appreciate the school, to learn with eagerness, to turn with hunger to my books.

It had been books which first gave me a look at life beyond Teheran, beyond the villages, beyond Persia. The summer that I was nine I had spent a part of my summer vacation with my dearest aunt—the wife of my religious uncle. My mother was busy and my aunt was lonely. During this summer I had explored in her very wonderful basement. In her basement was everything. Simply everything! Among the unexpected treasures that I discovered was a book of forty ancient Persian romances. I made the mistake of reading the first of these stories to my aunt. She invited two of her friends to visit with her and often I would read six or seven hours a day to the three women. Although my aunt had learned to read, she still read letter by letter, not thought by thought, and it was a slow, hard process for her. It was much easier to sit and listen to me.

When the book of Persian romances was exhausted we found others, some of them translations from the French. Sitting in that ancient home on the low bench of richly up-holstered Persian fabric with the three women listening for every word, we were four people, leaving our ancient country and living in a new and different land. I know now that it was desire for escape from the strict laws that regulated the life of my aunt that made her hungry for these books. The books were never in sight when my uncle was at home. I would escape with them and find some hidden corner to complete the story for myself.

My poor aunt! In the evening my uncle would ask about my froglike voice and she would make potions to clear away my hoarseness. Probably she felt a little guilty, but still she must escape in her mind at least from the day-after-day dreariness of her circumscribed life.

Back in school I thought often of the hours I had spent reading to my uncle's wife. Often I saw the books we were reading through her eyes and they took on even greater glamour. I tried to open my heart and mind as well as my eyes to the reading.

In Persia we have many of the classics of the Western world. In excellent translation we have the works of Victor Hugo. *Les Miserables* I loved to read over and over. Jean Val-jean was my brother. He knew hunger for bread as I had seen it in my country. He had made a life of giving, and he had improved the condition of those around him. To me he was a "religion man" of greater stature than the men who read the Koran in the church. I thought often of him.

And the dream that I had had of helping the people of the village came back to me. For a time I had almost forgotten it. I had been silly, I had not had sense, but now I was older.

There is something in the French temperament and the Persian temperament that is particularly congenial. Translations from the French are not word translations; they are something more.

Other books which I specially enjoyed in translation were *The Count of Monte Cristo* and *The Three Musketeers*. We also have an excellent Shakespeare translated by Hekmat, a poet who was once minister of justice and a fine philosopher. I liked best *Romeo and Juliet* because it is so romantic and because the marriage customs seemed to be similar to those of my country. I liked *Hamlet*, too, and *Macbeth*. My country is a land of violence and we can understand violence in literature. We have some translations of Dickens; we have the *Song of Roland*; we have Stefan Zweig and Abdullah. We have many translations from the Russian but those do not please me especially.

But even more stimulating to my mind and emotions were the works of Persia's own writers. Very few of our writers—our great writers—have expressed themselves in prose. In our country poetry is the natural expression. Perhaps it is because our people have not been a literate people. They have been unable to read, but they have had fine minds, good memories, and great sensitivity for beauty. What the poets have written the people have memorized and have taught their children from one generation to another. Perhaps it is because Farsi is a beautiful liquid language. I have been told that it is even more beautiful than Italian and not to be compared with the harshness of English. In our language we do not have a jolting combination of stressed and unstressed syllables, rather there is a softness in each syllable. Farsi is the language for poetry.

I do not mean pure Farsi. Reza Shah appointed a committee called the Farhang to take the Arabic out of our language and leave only the words of Farsi origin. We had been using a composite language for more than a thousand years and in this composite language all of our literature had been written. When we say Farsi we mean our enriched language just as you do when you say English.

It may be that poetry is our natural expression because we are a people who love design and poetry is writing with design. Or perhaps it is because we are a very sensitive people, with our hearts always ready to be played upon with deep ideas expressed in appealing words.

In America you do know a little of our literature. The *Arabian Nights* stories are of Persia and were carried West by the Arabs who left us the Koran and took with them not only our architecture, our art, but also our stories. But to me the *Arabian Nights*, rich though they are in fancy and in romance and adventure, are not our really great literature.

After I had returned to the advanced school the Persian magazine, *Mihre*, asked who is the best poet in Persia. The poets Firdausi, Mollavi, Haffiz, and Sadii were nominated. The readers of Persia could not name the greatest. Firdausi makes the ancient days exist again; Sadii expresses the greatest religious philosophy; Haffiz is a poet for everybody—every man, every woman, every boy, every girl, has a copy of Haffiz. The great poets of Persia are beyond discussion, are not comparable.

Firdausi was as great a writer as Homer, or Virgil, or Dante, or Shakespeare. His book which we call *Shah Namah* (Chronicles of the Kings) although it was written a thousand years ago still has much that is very deep and important to say today. But you know that. You have an excellent free translation of one of the Chronicles in Matthew Arnold's *Sohrab and Rustum*. At first it seems that this is a moving story of Rustum who dealt Sohrab a death blow before he recognized that the boy was his own son. Beneath the surface, it is the story of any person, any group, that goes blindly and stubbornly along a self-appointed path, never realizing that another course might avert sorrow and suffering. Rustum felt that he must save his reputation in spite of everything. That goal, alone, he could see; to all else he was blind. The reader, following the story of Sohrab and Rustum, thinks of blind masses of people, of blind political leaders, of blind nations.

That is the beauty and the challenge of Firdausi. I first read *Shah Namah* when I was thirteen. Since then I have read it three times. Each time it says more to me. I think I still do not understand half of what the poem has to tell me.

Very soon again I shall read it and see if my broader experience has made me more capable of understanding.

But in spite of the difficulty of understanding all of his thoughts from his words, there are some parts so simple that everyone can understand. In the bazaars and around home fires in the villages, his verses are recited by people who have never learned to read, but who have heard these verses from their parents who have heard them from their parents. They do not know that they quote poetry. They only know that the beauty is satisfying to their ears and to their hearts.

The Farsi of Firdausi is almost the Farsi of today; that is why we say that Firdausi "set" the Persian language as the King James version of the Bible set your English.

It is unfortunate that Persian poetry cannot be translated into English, really translated, I mean. It is a difficult thing to explain, of course, just why this can't be done. Maybe for the same reason that the Russian writing has not been well translated into Persian.

In a language of a people, especially an old people who have relied for thousands of years upon the spoken word, each word becomes more than a symbol. The word does not stand for a particular thing, either concrete or abstract. Rather it evokes a thousand ideas from the culture of the people, with which it clothes itself.

Because you have an excellent English poem, "The Rubáiyát of Omar Khayyám," which was taken from a poem written almost a thousand years ago by a Persian mathematician and astronomer, I will try to show you what I mean by quoting the most familiar lines from the FitzGerald poem.

> A Book of Verses underneath the Bough
> A Jug of Wine, a Loaf of Bread—and Thou
> Beside me singing in the Wilderness—

"A book of Verses" means more to the Persian than it does to most Americans, I think. It represents an opportunity to enter the mind, the heart, the emotions of another, through an ideal medium. Of course, there are some in America who will read the words "A Book of Verses" and feel the glow that the evocation of all of our racial love of poetry brings to a Persian on hearing the words. "Bough" suggests the image of a tree but it evokes a memory of Tree. Tree gives shade in the burning sun of an arid country; Tree promises that water is near; Tree symbolizes a life that successfully stands against twin enemies, aridity and sand. In the north where there is abundant rainfall and everything is green-green Tree does not mean all these things, but Omar was a desert poet.

"Wine" is not just something to drink. In the Moslem world where wine-drinking is forbidden, the word evokes an image of independence and adventure. "A loaf of bread" may mean lunch to the Western world; but in my country bread stands between man and death by starvation. "And thou beside me"—what special meaning this has when one realizes the emphasis on sexual love in Persian life.

If you could think of all these things as you read your Anglo-Persian poem you would have something of the feeling that Persians get from the reading of Omar.

Of the poets I think Haffiz is my personal favorite. In the first place his philosophy is right for me. May I quote from an English translation.

> In wide Eternity's vast space
> Where no beginning was, wert Thou:
> The Rays of all-pervading grace
> Beneath Thy veil, flamed on Thy brow.
> *Then Love and Nature sprang to birth*
> *And Life and Beauty filled the earth.*

And the final couplet:

> The world's possessions fade and flee,
> The only good is—loving Thee.

You will smile, but it is a custom in my country to use Haffiz as sort of a household prophet. He is so deep, yet so simple that he has words for everyone. When we are bothered with a problem we say, "God keep you, God give you Haffiz," and we take his book of poetry in our hands. Then we say, "Haffiz, would it be well for me to travel?" or maybe, "Haffiz,

is this the man my daughter should marry?" Then we open
the book just any place, and there is the answer. You will
smile, but many times even the words of our question are in
the answer from the book of Haffiz.

His poetry is exactly opposite to that of Omar Khayyám.
Omar felt that death was the end of all things; Haffiz says:
(I don't like this in English translation. It sounds harsh.)

> Since first I heard the blissful sound—
> I knew with thankfulness profound
> His sons we are—our Home is Heaven.

People who live in a land where death comes too often and
too soon need the comfort of Haffiz.

There are other excellent poets, too: Sadii; Jalal-ud-Din;
Nizami who was once the adviser to the king; Rudagi, whose
poetry glorified the king and had little feeling for the people;
Anvari; Farid-ud-Din.

Then there are the modern poets from whom I read little
when I was in school: Pishman-i-Bakhtiari; Bina; Shafaq, a
philosopher, Iranian patriot, and United Nations member
whom I once met and liked very much; Sarmad; and Lahuti
who thought that the best thing for our people is bread
through communism and who is now in Russia at the request
of the government of Persia.

It seems to me that as I think of the school now it is the
association with books, rather than the work of the teachers,
that opened new doors for me. Always I had a book with me.
Sometimes when the teachers were conducting classes I had
my book out of sight, reading it, or the ideas from a book in
my head, weighing them.

There are things about the Persian school that are good:

the thoroughness, for example. There are things which some-day I hope will be changed.

I would like to see a two-day-a-week free period as in America so that the home could take a larger part in the child's development. Especially in the high school I feel that provision should be made for the student to work part time. There are so many who can't afford school as it is, and such a provision would make an opportunity for these boys and girls. Then, too, there is very little taught in our school to prepare people for living. Sewing and design, yes, but nothing of sociology or psychology, or politics, or government, or vocations.

Every mind must sort out for itself that which is useful and that which has no place in it. This the mind will do if left alone. It is a bad thing, I think, to ask that everything that is taught must be remembered for the whole period of going to school with a great final examination on the whole always hanging like doom over the head.

In Persia there is no free speech, no chance for initiative in the schoolroom. We do not educate the children to take a place in a free world, a world that is free both politically and economically.

But most important, I would like to see a school in each village so education could be universal. The children in the school should be learning vocations as well as reading and writing and the cultural subjects. We need more of practical agriculture, of shoe mending, of home economics, of engineer-ing, of business.

And because I am young, I think it would be pleasant and wise for boys and girls to go to school together. But this my country will not do for many years, I am sure, although both men and women attend the University of Teheran.

When we have finished the work at the advanced school, we go to another school for the final examination. In Persia you are not examined on what you have thought nor on your reactions to what you have read. The examination is on *the book*. I cannot say that I was the best when I took this examination; but I was better than the average in memory. I knew a great deal that was not in the text because I was learning to use knowledge, to acquire it wherever I was.

There was one field of knowledge in which I had no interest. That was—what do you call it?—experimental biology? When I was visiting in Chalus we found a little dead bird. Of course I was too old to hold a funeral for it as I had for my hen. Sijavish rushed to the house and came back with his little very sharp knife. "I shall see what is inside," he said, going to work on it with his knife.

"No," I cried. "Don't do that!"

"It's dead, isn't it?" he asked. "I'm not hurting it. I'm learning something."

Sijavish was finding with the dead bird and his knife what I found in books. His way of learning made me sick at my stomach.

At the close of our school there is not the formal graduation exercises that you have in America with many speeches and special costumes. For those who passed the examination there was a large and very dull reception given.

"Hello. How are you? . . . Very well. . . . Thank you. . . . I have enjoyed the school, too. . . . Thank you."

Very dull!

The real happy hour of finishing the advanced school was in the giving of a benefit for people caught in a disaster. I do not remember what disaster. I wonder why? Perhaps it was because, though I was sorry about the disaster, I was most happy about the benefit.

All of the older girls were in the performance, dressed in robes of the palest blue very soft material. My robe was of white. As we put on make-up behind the scenes, we told each other that we looked like the beautiful women from the *Arabian Nights*.

I was alone on the softly lighted stage and the curtains opened. Before me the opera house was dark, but I knew that all of my family was out there hoping for me. I was not at all afraid as I began to sing the beautiful poem by Sadii called "The Caravan." This is a free translation:

> Go slowly and slowly and slowly, caravan.
> You take my heart with you.
> If I die people will find one thousand reasons.
> Only my heart knows my life.
> If my heart goes with you how can I live?

The other girls had come in behind me and now sang with me. For the first time I was conscious of the orchestra; the violins, the other soft stringed instruments.

After the song we all danced. I felt a special light on me bringing out the whiteness of my robe. If my life were different I would like to sing and dance forever, but this I can never do. Never can I dance or sing for money for myself. There was happiness in the audience because of our singing and dancing, and it flowed toward the stage like a great ocean and engulfed us.

While I was still reliving the night of the benefit, Mother said, "What are you going to do now? Now that you have finished the advanced school?"

"I have thought of the University of Teheran," I said,

though I hadn't thought seriously of it at all. Two thousand students from Teheran passed the examination from the advanced school. Of these two thousand there would be room for about four hundred and fifty in the University.

"I have thought, too, of going back to the school of design." Perhaps I would learn more there now I had matured; and it was the best school of fashion design in Persia.

"Must it be school?" my mother asked.

"For now it must be school," I said.

## · 9 ·

# THE WEDDING

IF A little person, three or four years old, maybe asks, "Who is God?" it is hard to answer. "God is a father that we cannot see," you say. "He is like your father. He loves you. He gives you many things. He watches over you. He wants you to be happy, but you must be kind and good and clean so he shows you how to be these things."

If the child has a good father that is the answer; but if the father is cruel, selfish, many times leaving the mother with hungry children dragging at her skirts, you have said nothing true about God.

But if you ask, "Tell me about the landlord in your country?" it is true to answer, "He is like a father." Sometimes he is like a bad father, caring nothing for the misery of his people, but sometimes he is different—kind and good, and thoughtful in providing the best for his people.

Such a landlord I knew in Kazvin.

The family was a very important family with many long names connected with it; but for short it was called the Monsoo family. Often the father of the family visited in my home when he was on business to the capital. Sometimes he brought with him his wife and his daughter, Shikuh.

Shikuh was someone special to me. She was older than I but we liked the same books and had similar ideas so she flattered me with her attention. She was tall, strong-boned, with a special forceful way of saying the things she believed. When Shikuh was to visit us there was nothing that would take me away from home.

One afternoon as the two of us sat in the court she said, "Najmeh, I'm going to be married."

"Married?" I asked. I knew that she was of an age for marriage but anyway I was surprised. I must have something to say so I asked, "Who is the man?"

I watched the color come up over her face and it seemed to me that the flesh softened to cover the strong bones with a sort of girlish roundness. Her smile was very sweet. "My cousin, Hoseh. Oh, you'll like him, Najmeh."

"Is he a man?" I asked.

"I do not want to marry a man," she said. "He is a boy." She laughed, a soft chuckle in her throat. "He is such a dear clown. But you will see. At first my mother was not satisfied, but I think now she is happy."

I went back to her earlier words. "When will I see him?"

She took my hand. "Najmeh, I want you to come to my wedding."

"Here in Teheran?"

"No, in Kazvin, of course. Our villages are all about Kazvin and I wouldn't be married without the people from our villages. They love me." She laughed again in her throat, "And they love a celebration."

We did not have much time for discussing the words of Abu

Said that visit. She had much shopping to do before she returned to Kazvin.

Six days before the wedding my mother put me on the train.
In Kazvin, Shikuh and her father met me. I was eager to meet
the boy and it wasn't long until I did. When we reached the
beautiful Monsoo home Hoseh was there. I knew at once why
Shikuh could feel love for him. He was short, wide and with a
round humorous face. There is an American word, "cute," that
might be fitting for Hoseh. He was very friendly with me at
once and when I saw the glances that passed between Shikuh
and Hoseh I was very glad that the mother had decided to be
satisfied with him. There was much warm love and sort of a
half-gay understanding, too.

The first night after dinner Hoseh started to tell a story. He
did not have the "once upon a time, maybe in another world"
story-telling sound of The Match. Instead he acted each part
as he told it. He was so funny. Shikuh's father held both arms
crossed on his stomach and shouted with laughter. The mother
laughed, too. I looked for a tightness about the mother's lips
but it was not there. If she had been against the marriage it
was not because she didn't like Hoseh. Sitting and eating you
could feel the joy in the room bathing you with its warm
currents.

The next day the mother took from the purchases she
had made in Teheran great lengths of fine material. Shikuh's
girl friends in Kazvin came very early and we began to sew.
We cut and made the white wedding dress, the slips, the brassieres, all of the dainty things the bride would need. Sometimes we talked of serious things, but mostly the talk was girl
talk. "Then he is saying—" "Then I am saying—" as in
America or any other place.

Always there were tea, fruit, sherbet, the best of bread, and cakes.

One afternoon Hoseh came to visit the family. We were tired of sewing. He let us make up his face with rouge, lipstick, pencil and put a flower in his hair. He looked more like a girl than Shikuh when he began the dance of the slave for our enjoyment.

Four days seemed like one day. The next day we went to the public bath, fifteen laughing, merry girls. All day we spent in the bath. There was a special expert to pluck our eyebrows, treat our lashes, there was the shampoo, the soothing rub with the bath mitten, the steaming that makes one clean clear to the inside, the plunge in the hot water and the sharp chill of the cold water as we went shrieking into it for only a moment.

During the last part of the bath there had been a band of musicians playing outside the bathhouse. Our instruments are different from yours, but there are strings and drums and cymbals. As we came out the village people and the people of Kazvin threw flowers and little white candies on the street in front of Shikuh's feet.

The next night two mullahs came for the marriage ceremony. In my country there are mullahs of different prices. If you are wealthy you may buy the best mullah for the occasion. If you are not, poor mullahs will marry you as tightly.

The house was beautiful for the wedding. In the court there were rugs covering the walks and hanging from the walls to make a rich room of deep tapestry. The court was spread for the men. In the women's room there were also very rich rugs, much beauty.

In Moslem weddings the bride, dressed in white and with a veil over her face, sits alone in a room close to the court, and close to the room for the women. She sits on the floor on a special piece of finest Persian pure silk with maybe threads of real metal worked into the design. Behind her is a mirror and tall candelabra. At each side there is a long piece of bread almost like a rug. You don't have anything in America like these very long pieces of flat bread, square at one end, the other end pointed. Into the bread, in beautiful Persian design, is placed colored incense for future burning.

Outside the door of the bridechamber the two mullahs stand one on each side, reading from the Koran. Two times the bride must not answer the questions of the mullah. At this time it is the custom of the boy's mother to bring a gift of gold to show that she is willing. Hoseh's mother is dead so a kinswoman brings the golden bracelets. Now Shikuh answers "Yes," and there is a squeal from all of the women at the celebration and a great clapping of hands from everyone. Two women of the family—women who have been especially happy in their lives—come and stand before the incense-covered bread. One has two cubes of sugar between her palms. As she rolls her palms together a thin stream of sugar falls upon the floor. The bride will be sweet to her husband. It is the best quality in women in my country. The other woman has needle and thread. She sews while she says she is closing the mouth of the new relatives.

In Persia the boy takes the bride to the home of his mother. Shikuh would go to the home of Hoseh. There are many who whisper that Shikuh is fortunate to be at once mistress of her house. It is hard, sometimes, for the young girl to go to the home of the mother-in-law, especially if there are other sons and their wives already in the home.

Then the groom is led into the bride's room and the two

are left behind a drawn curtain while the mullahs make the marriage papers. One is for the parents of the girl, one for the parents of the boy.

Outside the Monsoo home there is already the sound of much music and in only a moment Shikuh and Hoseh go out to receive the congratulations of the people of the village. The villagers are in the most beautiful native clothes. The men have white shirts, clean from the harsh-soap rubbing. But the

Coins on the hair of the village dancer.

girls are dressed in very full skirts of brilliant cotton—some of the skirts of Persian print, others of one color like yellow or scarlet or purple. The bodices, cut like jackets, are very tight, making the waist seem small and showing the curves of the breasts. Usually the women wear long braids of hair hanging over their shoulders, but for this celebration they have opened the braids and attached to the ends of their hair little metal bells, and gold- and silver-colored coins. When they whirl in the dance the skirts stand out straight from their waists showing their matching ankle-length cotton pantaloons; the hair with the ding-ding-ding of little bells is flung out, confined only slightly by the bright-colored scarf worn loosely over the head.

The older village people, and the wide-eyed children stand back, watching the young folks dance. Later they light incense furnished by the father and a blue-white smoke of dense sweetness rises over the crowd.

To each person Shikuh gives a piece of money. I do not know how much money she gives but very much. Her father has furnished enough money so that the people of the village can each buy some needed thing.

The next day to the Monsoo home come gifts from the people of Kazvin who attended the wedding. There are gifts from the people of the village, too: a sheep, a sack of wheat, other produce. These gifts Shikuh, because she is like her father, appreciates most, with perhaps a few tears.

She is a fortunate girl. Her father's gift to her is a beautiful home in Kazvin. Now she will have a home for herself and one for guests. Her mother's gift is land so that Shikuh and Hoseh will also be landlords.

I did not stay in Kazvin until the day that the groom came to get the bride and take her to his home. That would be weeks, even months, and I had to return to school.

In the school there was romance, too. I felt different about this romance because my friend Safire was my age, not somewhat older as Shikuh was. I felt that Safire had been a traitor to our volleyball team by growing up and falling in love. We had had such fun with the volleyball, playing, running, jumping, screaming. But now when we got together to play, the girls would rather sit in a tight little group and talk about marriage, bridal dresses, homes, boys. Mostly about boys.

Disgusted, I got up and ran around bouncing the ball myself. "Are you a boy or a girl?" Safire asked me, half cross.

"Well, one thing, I am not thinking of marriage," I said.

One day when we were alone Safire said to me, "Najmeh, I'm in love."

"You're what?" I asked.

"Let us go to your room."

My room was across the court from the room in which sat Safire's mother and my own. My mother had not known Safire's mother until we became friends at school; then the whole family had grown friendly. "I don't want my mother to know it. I'm in love."

"Have the suitors been to your home?" I asked.

"*He* wouldn't send suitors," she said with such scorn that I was surprised.

"Why wouldn't he?"

She paid no attention to my question. "Oh, Najmeh, what shall I do? I'm so in love."

By then I could see that she was meaning what she was saying. I looked at her. She was a very tall girl. She was not pretty, but maybe beautiful. Her manners were the best and she had a beautiful body as well developed as a woman though she was only fourteen.

"How did you become so in love?" I asked, really wondering.

Her voice dropped to a whisper. He was a coach at the athletic field in Teheran. He had noticed her. They had begun to talk together when they could. He was in love, too.

"Then why doesn't he send suitors?"

"Oh," she said impatiently, "you wouldn't understand."

Very often we sat together in my room, she saying, "He told me this—I told him that—" and I listening half taken up with the romance of it all and half disappointed that Safire was no longer a satisfactory companion to me.

At last one day she showed me a letter she had written to her father. The letter said that she would elope unless the parents gave their permission to the marriage. "Shall I give this to my father?" she asked.

"It's your paper and your father," I said.

"I knew you'd agree with me," Safire said, and she hurried home to leave the letter on the table for her father.

I do not know what the father did when he read the letter. All I know is Safire came to my house and threw her arms around my neck and said over and over again, "It worked! Oh, I'm so in love!"

It was summer vacation before the wedding day came. We had a great deal of time to get ready. I made myself a new dress and bought my first pair of heeled shoes. The day of the wedding Safire and I went together to the beauty salon and she had her straight hair made curly, her brows plucked away from the bridge of her nose. The beauty parlor made her look very pretty and much older. She looked old enough to leave volleyball behind her.

Looking at Safire's parents one would never have guessed that the suitors had not come in the regular way. Persians have so much pride that their hearts are never exposed. The courtyard was a thing of beauty with its many rich carpets. Over the pool in the center of the court a lattice of wood was built and on this was placed a great table under a beautiful handwrought cloth. On the table was every food imaginable. Oh, that delicious cherry sherbet! Around the edge of the court the men guests were seated at little tables and served by men servants. At the left of the court was a room busy with people going and coming with food. Behind the court was the salon in which the women guests were served by women. A reception room opening with an arch onto the court was the room for the bride.

Safire looked like a strange person to me, white veiled and dressed in white, as she sat on the strip of Persian tapestry between the two long pieces of bread. The incense on the bread at her left hand spelled a Persian word—you do not have an English equivalent. It means maybe "Congratulations," possibly "May everything be always the best for you." At the left the incense made a design that was, perhaps, symbolic of the fertile things that grow on the earth.

The mullahs who had come to read from the Koran and ask the questions of marriage were the very best. My school friends and I stood in the reception room with our faces close to three windowlike openings into the bride's room, watching the woman of her family who was rolling the sugar, the one who was sewing the mouth of the mother-in-law. And I wondered about the mother-in-law.

Now the mullahs read from the Koran. We could see Safire stand silently, and I remembered her saying, "I love him so much! What am I going to do?"

Again the question. Again silence.

Now the mother-in-law came with the golden gift. The mother-in-law of Safire gave a necklace. The mother-in-law was a beautiful woman, young and straight, and well poised. It was not true that the physical education coach was without family.

Now the bride said "Yes." Though we did not hear her we knew because the band struck up the special music, the women squealed, the men applauded. Into the air was thrown much confetti.

We did not hear because two of my friends and I had

slipped into the bride's room and hidden behind the curtain which had been pulled to cover the three windows we had been looking through.

We held the edges of the curtain together above and below our eyes and watched the male relatives of the groom escort him to the bride's room. Tall, handsome, wide shoulders, beautiful body! Then the curtain was pulled. Except for our prying eyes they were alone. What would they do?

The Wedding.

They cried. Both of them cried, tears running down their happy faces. They really were in love just as Safire said. They didn't kiss, nor touch each other, only cried. And we—stupid little children still—laughed. They jumped at the sound. The groom opened the curtain. Outside in the court there was more music and dancing had begun.

Safire stayed with her mother for the rest of the summer, preparing her dowry and listening to her mother talk about the duties and responsibilities of a wife and mother. Often I sewed with Safire and knew that she could scarcely wait to go to the home of the boy. Her mother had a copy of the mullah's marriage paper. The mother-in-law had a copy also. And Safire was eager to be really married.

"It will be very soon, now," she told me one day. And it

was so soon that I had to hurry to make another new dress, listening to my mother's grumbling about expensive new dresses when there were many I might wear.

On the day fixed upon, the dowry, arranged on great wooden trays, was carried by porters to the home of the groom. Two hundred porters and more! What a bag full of tips those porters would receive from the boy or his father!

I was at Safire's home when the knock came at the door. Knock, knock, knock. The mother began to cry. Surprisingly, Safire did, too. "Oh, Mother," she cried, her arms tight about the mother's neck. "It is good-by. It is good-by." And then my friend did not seem like the strange woman that had sat on the Persian tapestry in the bride room. She was a little girl who should be slapping a volleyball with a sharp, lifting-up stroke of a strong palm.

The door was opened and the groom's kinsmen waited for the bride. Outside were cars beautifully decorated with white flowers and ribbon. The bride was assisted into the first car still drying her eyes. The groom was there to take her hand and to smile at her foolishness. I, with my two friends, rode in the second car. There were other cars, too, carrying many friends. Everybody was going to the home of the groom but the parents of the bride who must stay in their own home and not enter with their daughter into her new life.

At the home of the groom Safire was laughing and happy again. There was dancing and eating—perhaps some drinking, though it is against Islamic law. At about twelve everybody watched the male relatives of the groom put the two together in the bridal room, then everybody went home, leaving them alone. This time my friends and I did not hide behind a curtain.

The next day everybody sent wedding gifts. My family and I sent a box of chocolates and flowers as something special with our gift of a length of fine Persian fabric. That afternoon we again went to the celebration at the home of the groom. At this party the bride wore flowers in her hair and a pink dress instead of white, to show that she was no longer a virgin.

I did not see Safire again for some time. When I went back to school I missed her. We needed someone next to the net tall enough to slap the ball directly down into the other court. I have not seen her often since. She is leading a very modern life. She has three beautiful children and both she and her husband are teaching physical education.

Sometimes the girls talked about Safire and her wedding; especially of her daring romance in the new fashion. I had enjoyed the excitement but I never thought of myself in her place. I was not grown up enough to want marriage for myself. I spent much of my time in daydreaming, but my dreams were more of remote things than of something very close and very possible—very much what would have made my mother happy.

Very often from that time I went to weddings. Some were like Shikuh's, some in the city like Safire's. Some were Western-like weddings. In these the mullahs married the couple very quietly in the home and the reception was held with Western music, ballroom-type dancing, food and liquor at some hotel, or if the affair were really important at the Officers' Club which Reza Shah established in Teheran. Here four or five thousand guests could be entertained at once.

Sometimes my mother spoke to me carefully about marriage, and my sisters spoke of marriage to me more plainly. But the desire had not come to me. Kismet—Fate—had other ways for me to walk.

CHAPTER

· 10 ·

# THE TOO FREQUENT VISITOR

I WAS thirteen—or maybe fourteen when I first came close to the most frequent visitor, the most unwelcome visitor in my country or any other—Death.

My father had died before I knew him, my mother had lost three children of her family of eight and would have lost me had it not been that Zarah's baby died and left my kind nurse with a full breast to offer me. But still I had no memory of Death's coming. I had that wonderful indestructible feeling that I think most young people have. Death is for others, never for us. Perhaps it is this conviction that although people around us may die, we, blessed especially, shall go on forever, which makes young people take long chances in cars, on skiis, in mountain climbing.

I had reached thirteen and Death was a stranger to me.

One evening after I was in bed the telephone summoned my mother. A relative of hers had died in Teheran. Mother dressed and went at once, leaving instructions for me to come to my aunt's home in the morning.

Even before I reached the courtyard I heard wailing

from inside. My kinswoman's children had returned to their mother's home during the night and already friends were calling to console them. There was no attention paid to me but at last I was told that my mother was in the bedroom of my aunt. Everywhere in the house there was crying. "Already the morning prayer has been said," I heard as I went up the stairs from the corridor. "It is soon time for the mullah to pronounce the noon prayer."

My mother was just inside the arched doorway to the bedroom. She put an arm around me and led me in to the bed on which my aunt lay. She was a very beautiful woman, and even in death she retained that look. There was no make-up on her face, no jewelry at her neck or ears or wrists, but still there was the look of fulfillment on her face. I looked about me at the other faces in the room. Every face was bloated and puffy from crying. Only the woman who had quit this life was happy.

It was time for the noon prayer. We bowed facing Mecca and heard quite clearly the words of the mullah: "Forgive her. Guard her soul. God accept this believer, this clean woman." Then the sound of mourning rose again.

After a time I went but my mother remained in the home of her relative. Missing my mother, and somehow liking the excitement of the house of mourning, I went back and forth between my home and the home of my relatives many times. No one paid attention to me. I went and came as I pleased. After a few hours the body of my aunt was placed on a sort of litter and carried to a special car, similar to your hearse. I understood there had been an argument about whether the body should go by car or be carried by many men. She was rich and famous for her kindliness and for her beauty, but after all she was a woman! Her body was taken by car. Before this car went another large car loaded with flowers. Behind there was a long procession of cars. Our chauffeur was there to take my mother, one of my sisters and her husband, and me. Slowly the procession moved to a special place for the washing of the body. Here the cars stopped and the mourners gathered for prayer and for crying. Again we heard the mullah's prayer. "God forgive her. God guide her soul."

After a time the body, washed and wrapped for burial, was brought out of this place and slowly, slowly the procession moved toward the cemetery. When we left our cars at the cemetery I saw my aunt again. Now the body was wrapped in the best Persian material. Across the eyes there was a band of muslin to close them. The hands were bound to the sides by another strip of muslin around the wrists and the feet were bound together at the ankle. When the mourners saw the body wrapped in this way the surge of sound rose, and through its uneven, sorrowful music there were little sharp edges of hysterical, uncontrolled crying. This continued while the body was lowered into the ground.

In Persia there is no vault, no coffin. The Koran says that the body is to be returned to the dust. Over the face is placed a sort of three sided box so that the covering dirt will not be dropped on that part of the body.

A great wail arose as the earth was dropped in to cover the body. My mother held me more tightly and looking up into her face I thought, "This might be my mother," and only then did the tears come to my eyes.

After the burial the procession returned to the home of my aunt. Here for three days the Koran was read by a mullah who came to comfort the family. Again I went back and forth at will. There was a great cloth spread in the dining room and on it was every variety of excellent food: fruit, bread, cheese, cakes. At the end of the three days the oldest son who was now the head of the house, folded the cloth as a sign that the mourning was finished.

After seven days my mother called her chauffeur to take us to the cemetery. There, near my aunt's grave, a cloth was spread. The mullah was there reading the Koran and preaching while people ate and cried.

After forty days we again went to the home to do honor to the dead and offer sympathy to the living. Again there was mourning. A year passed and there was a gathering in the cemetery again and one in the home that those who sorrowed could eat, and cry, and be comforted.

Often during the year I thought of the death of my aunt. I had loved her and admired her, and I felt sorry for my mother who seemed sincerely to mourn, but the whole thing, all of the feasting and crying, and reading of the Koran, seemed like a pageant to me. It reminded me of Moharram. Then I wondered if there was something wrong with me that I did not cry with the others. Perhaps I had an unnatural heart.

I had felt a stirring of pain when I saw my kinswoman wrapped for burial, when I had seen the dirt fall upon her and cover her. Those two things had made me feel the reality of our parting from her. And I thought of the custom of the Parsees of our country.

The Parsees are Zoroastrians whose customs are very different from the Islamic customs of the Moslems. They believe that everything in the world is either good or bad and there is a sharp line between the evil and good; the two must never

mingle. Earth and fire are both good, but the physical body
of man, as contrasted with the firelike spirit that animates
it, is evil. Since the good and evil cannot be mingled, the
dead body cannot be consumed by fire or put into earth. The
dead of the Parsees are dressed in their most beautiful clothing, their hair is oiled and dressed, they are adorned with
jewels. Then they are taken into the cemetery and set upon
sort of a wooden throne and left there until they decompose.

I have not seen a Parsee funeral. Sometime, perhaps I may.

I was on a vacation to the south, visiting a kinswoman in
the city of Abadan, when I first was really impressed by Death.

I was standing on the balcony of my aunt's house looking
down into the court and planning with a part of my mind to
visit the people of that region who live in tents, coming and
going with the seasons, when I heard a strange, not quite
human noise. Sort of a keening, it was—a closed off kind of
crying.

I went down a step or two toward the court, and then I
stopped. I would be an intruder at the pool. Kneeling beside
it was a woman, her thin, dark veil falling over her face. She
was washing a child. I could see her hands go gently over the
long thin limbs. The child was perhaps nine or ten, very long
he seemed, and slender. Why did not a child of ten wash
himself? Or perhaps he was sick. Then abruptly I knew and
wondered why I had not known before. The child was dead,
and the mother, here at the pool alone, was preparing him
for burial.

Tears burning in my eyes, but not falling, I watched her
every slow motion. When she washed the cheek she laid her
own cheek against it and her keening rose a little higher—
but still not loud enough to be called crying. With her fingers

she straightened the damp locks of his hair. Folded beside her was a worn piece of muslin that once had been a part of a full skirt. She shook it out, laid it on the walk beside the pool, and carefully placed the body on it. Then she folded the blue cotton garment she had taken from the body. Tomorrow a living child would wear the clothing of the dead. To do anything else would be waste.

From somewhere in the shadows a tall boy of perhaps sixteen or seventeen approached her and knelt down beside her. I had talked to this boy when I had first arrived. His name was Hassan, and I had talked to him of the city dwellers who are poor as the villagers and asked him if the people of Abadan were hungry. He had answered with fierce pride that they had bread and leek and tea. With him he had brought a net and he wrapped the child in the cotton cloth and laid it on the net. Before he rose he put his arm around the shoulders of the woman. Then the two of them lifted the net, one at each end, and carried it away.

Quietly I hurried down the steps, across the court and onto the street. We were not far from the river. I followed them at a little distance until we reached the river. They crossed it, carrying the little body, and I went back to the balcony, thinking and crying. The two would dig a grave somewhere across the river and put the child into it. Across his face they would put a strip of the muslin so that dirt would not fall upon his features; then they would fill the grave and go home. No funeral, no special prayer, nothing. Only death.

Often the mother in the evening when her work is done will go to the mound that covers her boy. She will weep in this strange, quiet, constrained fashion. If only she could scream wildly so that her grief could be thrown out into the waiting winds. But she cannot. I am glad that she will have the son, Hassan, to comfort her.

I had returned to Teheran when I heard that this older boy, too, had died, of the hunger.

I have heard that the average woman of thirty in my country has had ten children and that between five and six have survived. I do not know if this figure is correct. There is no way to know for sure since statistics are not kept carefully in many places; but I believe it is true. There is so much hunger.

One American woman asked me, "Since your people know this is so, do they take death for granted? Isn't it easier on them than on people like us?"

"Easier?" I say, thinking of the keening mother washing her dead child at the pool. Easier when added to the sorrow of parting is the feeling that the death need not have been at all if she, herself, could have done something. If she could have put food into a starving body, perhaps. There are so many babies that die in the villages. The mother, underfed herself, and working from dawn until darkness in the fields, does not have enough milk. She dips a clean cloth into goat or cow milk and offers it to the child to suck. Perhaps he will survive, perhaps not. And then the mother will say over and over again in her heart, "If I could only have given him a full breast! If I—"

After I had heard of the death of the boy, Hassan, I thought often of the shortness of life. Gone was the feeling of indestructibility. I knew that sometime I would die. That if by accident I had not been born into a family where want was a stranger I might even now be dead. When I read the Koran daily to my mother, I turned so often to the Suras about death that she must have wondered:

Every soul shall taste of death, and ye shall have your rewards on the day of Resurrection; and he who shall be far removed from hell fire, and shall be admitted into Paradise shall be happy; but the present life is only a deceitful provision.          Sura 3:185.

God gives you life; and afterwards causeth you to die: hereafter will He assemble you together on the day of Resurrection; there is no doubt thereof; but the greater part of men do not understand.

Sura 45:24.

It is well, I think, that the people that I love are clean. That there is a God who can love them and bring them finally to a better life. But I cannot believe that God "causeth you to die" even though that is what the Koran says. I know that Death comes more often to the villagers than need be, and I feel that the lack of understanding—perhaps the greed—of some men "causeth [others] to die."

I am reminded of a story about Alexander the Great. In our country he is known as Alexander with the Golden Horn— Dhu'lkarnein—and there are many, many legends about him. It is said that his mother and both of his wives were Persian so he belongs to us. In this story Alexander had died and was prepared for the burial but no band of muslin could hold his hand at his side. As soon as it was bound it would free itself, and bent like a cup would reach out from the litter on which the body was carried. "His soul cannot rest until the hand is filled," the wise men said. And everybody sought to find what the hand wished to hold. Into it went many riches, gold, sapphires, rubies. But never was the hand satisfied. At last a poor old man picked up a fistful of sand and put it into the cupped hand. The fingers closed around the sand and the hand was content to be bound. Only the dust of the grave is ours after death, the legend says.

But still there are many in my country who prefer to fill their hands with the riches of the world—and many who die for want of bread alone.

There must be an answer. I must find it.

Nobody knows when the rich sin.
Nobody knows when the poor die.

# THE VILLAGE

I T WAS the Islamic New Year. In Teheran the gardens were beginning to flower and the purple faces of wild violets lifted from the most unexpected places. It was a New Year and a holiday.

"Let's," said my friend Nahete, "have a real holiday! Let's go to the mountains in the north for four days of skiing."

"Skiing?" I asked. "But New Year's is to celebrate the going of winter. Why should we look for some more?"

Nahete laughed. "A four-day holiday would be fun. Ali (she named her husband) is eager to go and we can get Fateh and Hassan to go, too." She drew a long face. "If only you were married, Najmeh, it would be perfect. The six of us."

It would never have occurred to us in Persia to ask an unattached young man to be my partner for the four days even with this double chaperoning. It isn't done.

"But I'm not married. I—"

"Najmeh, we'd be staying in a village. You could—"

She knew my interest in the village. She knew that every time I had a chance I visited some village not too far from

Teheran. She watched my face and pressed the point. "This would be a different sort of village. You could see how people live over there."

We hurried to consult a map. The snow country was in Azerbaijan. We could go as far as the city of Zenjan by train. From there we could go by horse and if the snow were deep we'd finish our journey by ski, carrying our packs on our backs. Because we intended to travel by horse and by ski, we would take as little as possible. We could not go to a village without carrying a gift, but a mutton we would buy at Zenjan.

Since we were late in making our decision to travel there were no first- or second-class accommodations left on the train. This pleased me since I thought I would have an opportunity to become acquainted with villagers traveling short distances along the way. However, I was disappointed. Our third-class train was filled with other vacationers, many of them rich and haughty.

The trains are Western trains; riding in them is like traveling in America. For a time we passed through spring-tinted country but soon we came to the snow. Rolling hills and gradually rising mountains were snow sheeted. From my window the sky looked amazingly blue—a bright, almost dark blue that is much used in the enamel work of my country. The snow, reflecting it and reflecting the clear, light yellow sunlight, was not really white; rather it seemed to be almost a pale lavender, but very sharp and bright.

At the first train stop children's voices were raised in a shrill clamor. A woman across from me leaned across her husband to see out. "What?" she screamed, in answer to a request from outside. "Go away! Dirty!" The woman was well dressed in a suit designed especially for her, as is worn always by the well-to-do in Persia. But when her mouth opened to scream through the window she was the ugliest person I've ever seen. Hard eyes, a wide open mouth whose lower lip seemed to turn to the east while the upper lip pulled to the west.

I went out to the platform. Children had descended upon the platform like a swarm of locusts. And what pitiful children. Under the round brown wool caps of the boys and the frazzled head scarves of the girls were pinched faces burned red by the reflection of sun on snow. They all wore a sort of smock which had at one time been white—the girls' a little longer than the boys'—and pitiful slacks which ended in tatters just below the thin knees. One little boy held up his hand very close to me. His red-brown arm was practically out of the ripped sleeve of his blouse and it semed to me that I could see the bones move under the desiccated flesh.

I took from my purse all the coins I had and put them into his grimy, clawlike little hand. Immediately I was the center of a begging group—but I had no more to give.

After about fifteen minutes the train moved on. All I could see was the red-sore faces of those children, the great stomachs distended by famine. My heart was sick inside me. I couldn't stand to look at the woman across from me who had looked out of her window and not been touched by the need and the suffering.

There were other stops, other hordes of pitiful children, more crying inside me to find daily bread and more for my people.

We had been gone from Teheran a day and a half before we reached the tiny village where we were to stay. We were almost upon it before we saw it. Snow everywhere, the flat roofs of the brown houses scarcely above the level of the snow and tunnels into the doorways of the houses. There was no dirt anywhere. Beautiful world. White, clean world.

We went at once to the home of the headman. He was a pleasant man whose thin lips seemed carved to a smile and whose black eyes were lively and talkative. He spoke to us in Persian, so far removed from Farsi that it seemed almost a foreign language. Yet I understood him. Suddenly I realized that his Persian was more nearly Turkish than Farsi and I replied in my little Turkish. As soon as I spoke his smile grew wider and his eyes softer and warmer, though still keen and lively.

I looked around the room. The bricks that make the outside walls of such homes also make the inside—just opposite sides of the same sun-dried brick. But in this home there was a different decoration. Evidently this headman could read and took a newspaper from Zenjan. The room was papered with pictures cut from the papers; hardly a bare brick was visible. All around the room there was a sort of plate rail and on the rail there was a collection of treasures—empty glass bottles of many sizes and shapes; a few dishes; a mirror that had been capable of reflecting what was before it once upon a time, perhaps. But it was a warm room, a lived-in room.

We gave him the mutton to distribute to the people; he protested that no one was in need, but gave thanks for the mutton.

After the others had gone to ski I made friends with some of the children playing on the stiff crust of the snow. I noticed that their stomachs were distended like those of the children at the train stops. I talked to them and offered them the dates that I had brought in my pack. From them I found that of every three homes in the village only one had enough bread.

When I went back to the home of the headman there was lunch made for me. I wondered if he had put on for me his last bread but I did not ask. My people are proud people. To crush their pride is worse for them than the physical hunger.

"It has been a long hard winter," I said, as I sipped scalding tea fresh from the samovar.

"Yes," he said.

"How many people in the village?"

"About two hundred counting the females and the babies." Then he laughed at the teasing face I made him. In Persia women are not counted on the census for taxation or for any other purpose that I know of. He was just saying that the figure he gave me was not an official figure.

*One mutton and a handful of dried pease, a little rice and a few dates for two hundred people.*

When Nahete and Fateh and their husbands came in bringing a great cold and laughing noise with them the headman said, "Perhaps you would all like a bath." He showed us to the steam bath, we girls first, then Ali and Hassan. How good the water felt, and the all-enveloping steam. The bath was small. In this village where charcoal or wood would have been very difficult to get, the water was heated by the burning of dried dung. There were no bath attendants as in Teheran and no noise and laughter.

After the bath we returned to the headman's house and his family came in very quietly to meet us. We all sat down on the floor together to a meal of cheese and bread and milk.

"There is another hour or two of light. Come ski with us," Nahete begged me but I did not want to join them on the smooth slopes.

Sitting with the headman we were both silent, There was so much that I wanted to ask him, yet I did not want to step on his pride.

Finally I said tentatively, "Is the soil poor here? The water scarce?"

"The soil is not poor and melting snow makes plenty of water if we keep it in a lake behind mud walls until we need it. But the growing season is short and the landlord—"

"The landlord?" I questioned as he seemed reluctant to go on.

"One man owns this entire village. I do not know when he was last here. Maybe never. He does not know the condition of the people. This year has been harder than most, but most years are hard."

"Where does this man live?"

"Tabriz, I have heard, Teheran, perhaps. I have heard, too, that he has just one daughter on whom he lavishes everything. What she spends for adornment would feed several of these frugal families."

I was silent. I knew the law of the land: A fifth to the land, a fifth to the water, a fifth to the seed, a fifth to the ox, and a fifth to the laborer.

He knew that I was thinking of the law, I suppose, because he said, "Really the laborer gets more than one fifth here. Some own their own oxen." Then he sighed and his tight lids covered his bright eyes. "But if one owns the ox it must eat before the family to save its strength."

My Turkish which had been faltering at first now began to come back to me and I spoke with him more fluently. "May I visit in the homes of the village?" I asked.

"You love people?" he said with that warm live look in his eyes.

"I do love people."

His wife in a full-skirted dress of dark blue, her veil pushed back from her black hair, made tea for us, half listening to our conversation. "It is the long cold months," she said, bending over the samovar.

"Yes," the headman agreed. "So many idle months."

So many idle months, I thought. Yes, the quiet, busy wife of the headman was right. If only there were something useful to do during those long cold months. "There are the carpets," I said.

The headman nodded, the woman poured the tea into small glasses for us. "There are other things, too. The carding of wool, for example." He nodded his head toward the door of his living quarters and his wife, interpreting the nod, brought out her carding combs and wool. She carded by hand by drawing two boards with teeth of sharp wooden pegs across each other. First the left hand moving, then the right. He watched her for a time, his dancing eyes quiet and liquid with affection.

"But carpets and carding and spinning are not enough?" I asked.

"We must buy sugar and tea," he said. "Sometimes rice."

I sipped my tea, holding the glass in two cupped hands. An idea was growing with me. If there could be some way of earning money in the winter then the village people could cure their own suffering. Gifts of food—food is eaten in a day. Much better would be the gift of a way to earn food.

When the others came in from a day of skiing I was still sitting before the fire talking with the headman in my poor Turkish.

At bedtime I went into the home of the headman's family just behind the large room where he had entertained us. Here

I prepared a pan full of rice and dried peas and seasonings. I had brought these things with me. The children ate joyously. "Not every month, maybe every three or four months, we have rice," they said.

That night we all slept in the home of the headman. In the center of the room was a charcoal brazier. On each side of the brazier was a quilted cotton pad. We slept on these, our feet to the fire, covered with quilted pads almost as thick as those we slept on. There are very few beds in Persia. In homes that have felt Western influence there are beds, but other people are happy and warm and comfortable on the ground.

The next morning when I awakened the others were still sleeping. Quietly I went to the door and looked out. There had been a fresh snowfall over the old frozen crust during the night. From where I stood I could see the gentle toe tracks of some little bird across the new snow. From my bag I took pencil and paper and wrote a little verse in Farsi. The verse I wrote said: The little bird is hunting for something to eat. Perhaps he will find it. But the little children, where are they? They cannot find food in the snow.

When my companions awoke they could scarcely wait to get their skiis and be off. Again I decided not to ski with them. Instead I went with the headman to visit the homes of the villagers.

It was as I had guessed. Of every three homes only one had enough bread. But in every home bread was offered me. Bread for the children and for the guest, even where there is none for the adults of the house. We saw many women working at the carding and some at the spinning. In the village there are few spinning wheels. Most women work without even this aid. I saw the weaving being done on crude looms. The light reflected from the snow shines through the doorways of the houses and allows some inside work.

At one home I saw a woman washing. She was rubbing the stiff cotton of her family's clothes between her bleeding knuckles. The family remained in bed while the washing was done. For some time I watched her. She, like others in the village, needed a gift. Not an automatic washer, not a washer of any kind. A corrugated scrubbing board on which to rub the clothes would mean ease and luxury to her.

In the village, the headman told me, there were two young girls who had just become betrothed. Would I like to see them?

Yes, I said, wondering about dowries in this village of want. One of the girls was shy with me, but the other, a child of about eleven, came to me at once and put her arms about me. I looked at her laughing face, the dazzle of white fine teeth behind full, short lips, her black, charcoal-black eyes; and I thought what beauty she has! We made friends at once; she asking me questions so fast that my tongue tripped in answering them.

She conferred with her mother in Turkish-Farsi so fast that my ear could not follow her; then the two turned to the headman. He nodded, smiling.

As we walked back to the home of the headman he told me that the child had asked that a part of her wedding celebration might be moved up especially for my benefit. So sweet. So sweet an idea.

That afternoon the people of the village gathered in the snow outside the headman's home. The girls in their blue and white and red did many dances, some of which were strange to me because costume and folk dance are different in the different provinces. How brown the little brides looked in that dazzling whiteness. I myself have light brunet skin, light, sometimes golden, brown eyes, and hair of almost chestnut color. These girls were truly dark, almost brown. How happy the girls were; the boys, perhaps nineteen or twenty, very quiet and retiring on the edge of the crowd.

I went to my pack and found my complexion soap. I had not come prepared for a wedding. The soap I gave as a gift to the girls. The fragrance enchanted them. They thanked me again and again. Good soap may be made from tallow and the lye soaked from wood ashes, but to use it on tender skin is no luxury.

"But you have no soap left for yourself," the friendly little bride said sadly. "Look," I said, "if you have but one piece of bread you give it to me. Is that not true?"

She nodded.

"If I have but one piece of soap— Is it not right?"

Again she nodded, lifting her charcoal eyes to me with such adoration that I was ashamed.

"The people already love you. You must come back," the headman said.

"I will come back," I said, dreaming many nebulous, half-formed dreams in my waking mind. "You people have taught me many things."

On the way back Nahete and Fateh could talk of nothing but the skiing, laughing together about the mishaps, poking fun at Hassan who had been less skillful than the others.

I smiled at the proper times when their comments were addressed to me; but I was folded in thought. The people and the headman had taught me much, but now I must sort out the things they had taught me to make a pattern which I could carry in my mind.

Of course I could not go often to this village in Azerbaijan. But I could go more often to the villages closer to the railroad. I could take the things I had learned with me to make an understanding of other villages easy.

My mistake was, I found, to have gone to these other villages for only a few hours and then returned to Teheran. To know the villages and the people I must stay longer. I must live with the people, I must lie down at night on the dirt floors of their cottages with them and must eat around the samovar in the smoke-filled little rooms.

After that I went often to the villages, staying only a day sometimes, but during vacation time living for several days with the people in their crowded cottages, sleeping with them on their earth floors. For these journeys I did not pack a suitcase. I wore simple clothing, and like the people of the villages, kept my dress on day and night. I did not want to be different from them—a guest.

The people, who were at first distant, soon accepted me and hid nothing from me. I saw the life of the fellah more clearly with every visit. I understood the life more clearly than the people themselves, because they had nothing to compare and contrast with their harsh days and comfortless nights. I understood it more clearly than most people of the cities because for these scattered days I actually lived it.

I have watched the women grinding the wheat and have coaxed them to let me take a turn at dragging the rock across the indentation in the larger rock which holds the wheat.

Push, pull, push, pull and the grain is ground into an uneven meal that makes the best bread in the world. In the large villages a water mill may grind the wheat for everybody. Here the men will carry their sacks of wheat and laugh and talk together while the wheat is being ground by the moving stones powered by the water on the wheel. A part of the flour will belong to the miller, a part to the bringer of the wheat. It is good flour, but not so good as that which is ground by the women.

In the summer I have seen the women make this flour into bread. It is not at all like Western bread. It is very thin like your crackers but not at all of the nature of crackers. These long strips of very thin bread are dried in the summer sun. In the winter they can be dampened for use and will grow soft and delicious again.

I have seen the women making cheese from milk of the cow or milk of the goat. I have seen them dry fruit and hang grapes so that the raisins will be plump and soft and delicious.

I have eaten with these people. A little rice, a little wheat, maybe an egg for a special treat since many villagers keep a few chickens that are like members of their family. There is generally milk and sometimes cheese. The people love meat and can afford very little. The Koran allows them to eat beef, mutton, and wild game. In the lower villages the only obtainable meat is the mutton. At first I tried to take gifts of mutton with me wherever I went. Later I found that this was not a good idea. I did not want to be known as the dead-sheep woman. In the mountain villages there is more meat because hunting is good.

I have gone to the bathhouses of the village where most of the villagers pay with produce. I have sat in the steam and watched mothers with their whole flock of little children enjoying the warmth and the companionship of the bath. I have listened to their conversation and my heart has been about to break at the sadness, at the hopelessness of their talking.

Often in the bathhouse the talk is of the two years that each young man must spend in the army.

"Zeinab's baby is blind," says one woman. "It would be better if the little thing were dead but she will give it to suck, crying over it all the time."

"Allah Akbar—" another woman begins but the first shakes her head.

"It is not by decree of God," she says. "It is the disease. Hassi goes to the army. He is not wise. He needs women. His small money allows him no choice. He buys his satisfaction where it is for sale cheap. His two years are over and he comes back and marries Zeinab. The baby is blind."

The other woman turns her hands out in a gesture of hopelessness. "What is to be done?"

"What is to be done?" the first woman repeats.

And in my heart I say, "What is to be done?" I know that there is now Western medicine for this terrible disease, but I know the men of my country. They are the lords, they are the masters. Many of them, especially those who are ignorant, cannot be bothered. If only the salary of the common soldier in the army were large enough so he could marry before he left the village and take his wife with him. But then I am not wise. That might not be the answer.

"My Ismail has never come home. He likes the city too well. Or maybe he is dead. Who knows?"

And so the talk goes on about the two years of military service and I am sad. There is nothing I can do; no comfort I can offer.

Sometimes the talk is of other things. Gay things. There is

the village dolt who has gotten into some foolish trouble. There is here, as everywhere else, a fond retelling of the bright antics and comments of the children. There are jokes about the men of the village.

But mostly the talk is serious, sometimes sad.

When I leave the bathhouse my body is clean but I feel that my heart is not. There is too much sorrow in the world and I am as yet doing nothing to allay that sorrow.

Often I have looked into the churches where the mullahs— religious leaders who pass their positions on from father to son—read from the Koran and talk about the martyrs, the Imams, and other things pertaining to religion. I have seen the little boys going to mektab to learn a little of reading and writing; but in most village mektabs there is no one to teach the girls. It is not important that they must remain illiterate.

I have watched the men working in the fields, their blue cotton trousers rolled above their knees, and their white shirts stuck with sweat to their backs, their wide brown feet planted familiarly in the earth. It would be hard to pick the young men from the old, since all have faces burned dry by the sun shining redly under their brown wool caps, if it were not that the old are bearded and the young are shaven.

Beside the men are the women, veils over their heads and their skirts barely above brown ankles. Under the skirts are ankle-length trousers. Sometimes the dresses are of the same dull blue as the men's clothing; sometimes scarlet or saffron yellow skirts make bright splashes in the fields.

I have seen a woman, enormous with child, leave the field and return only an hour or two later with the child wrapped in a long narrow strip of cotton cloth. She will put the new-born mite in a sheltered place at the end of the row and look upon it each time she reaches that place in her planting, her weeding, or her harvesting. It is hard to believe but it is so. Sometimes I have seen a woman sitting between the rows, a child at her breast; other times I have seen her wearily dragging along a toddler, dressed like the mother with skirts to the ankles, hanging to her and crying and coaxing for care.

Why, I say to myself, can't these men have better tools so that they may work more quickly and the women have time for bearing and caring for the family? They do not need harvesters of the American kind, not tractors, not large farm machinery; just steel ploughs to be drawn by the ox, instead of wooden ones, just steel shovels, rakes, hoes.

I have watched the oxen walk back and forth on the threshing floor, walking the wheat out of the chaff and have seen the men throw the yellow straw into the air so that the wheat might fall out and be picked up by the women. It is a beautiful sight if one does not see the tired straining muscles, the perspiration-beaded upper lips and foreheads of the men. In some villages oxen do not tread the grain. Rather it is threshed by a very ancient machine—a long wooden roller with spikes arranged spirally on it, which is drawn by oxen.

People have asked me why the soil of Persia is not worn out after thousands of years. I do not know the whole answer. I do know that the great farm is farmed in strips, the strips being allocated to a different man each year. Crops are rotated. Manure, ashes, refuse are used for fertilizer. In my country, as in China, human excrement is not carried away to be wasted. It is deposited in trenches and later used for the enrichment of the soil. For this purpose it is the very best.

I have been asked, too, about the water. In my country

there is a very ancient system of carrying water from the place where it first comes out of the earth to the place where it is needed. We have underground channels called *kanats* or *quanats* through which the water flows. This is good. No one can steal the water, not even the sun through evaporation. Keeping the kanats in order is a big job, but there are many to do these jobs. There has been talk of great dams, like your Boulder or Hoover dams, for my people. I think that these would cost very much money and be of less value than smaller reservoirs connected with villages and cities by our own kanats.

Down the streets of the city, as well as through the villages, runs water, either underground or on the surface, which is used for all purposes except drinking. For drinking, water is purchased from a man who takes it where it first gushes forth and puts it into jars for our use. These jars are sometimes carried on the sides of donkeys. Great jars of water and little donkeys! It reminds me of the way the "little" men of my country are carrying great burdens.

Wheat is really the staple crop in my country, since it furnishes eighty per cent of the food my people eat. But there is another crop, too. A crop beautiful and dangerous.

You have not seen beauty unless you have gazed across a field brilliant with scarlet poppies which starts at your feet and stretches away to an unbelievably blue sky. There is always some wind in Persia and when it blows across this poppy field the poppy heads bow in turn and it is like the slow rolling wave on a crimson sea. Such beauty!

In each poppy stem there is a stream of sap that will bring good returns if sold to the government monopoly—much better returns if it can be hidden away and sold to an underground agent. These are the opium poppies, and their twelve per cent morphine content is the highest in the world.

When it is time to harvest the crop, men and women and children move into the field, careful not to destroy a single poppy. With a sharp knife a slit is made in the stem. That is all for today. Just a short, clean split. But tomorrow when the workers come again, out of this slit will have oozed the sap into a sticky gummy mass. It is now time to gather this gum for sale to the government or to smugglers.

Now there is no pleasure in the beauty of the field. It is hot, back-breaking work pulling the sticky gum from the stems. Beside the mother in the field is her baby, crying because he is hot and tired and hungry. The mother lifts him, gives him her sticky finger to chew upon. In a few minutes he is asleep and she puts him down again. The children beg for care. A sticky finger to suck upon for a few minutes and they, too, are happy. In the eighteen of our twenty-six provinces where opium is grown, it is used this way by even the tiniest children.

At first I was impressed with the beauty of the field, then I thought of the money this crop would bring to my country. It was later, when I thought of the little brown baby sucking hungrily upon the mother's opium-covered fingers that I felt concern. I did not blame the mother. She did not know. And was the baby not hungry? What could she do?

At home in Teheran between my visits to the villages I thought of the farmers, of their hopelessness and helplessness. They are patient, frugal, hardworking. Yet theirs is the existence of animals. If I think hard I can remember laughter ringing out over the fields—laughter or singing. I can remember the greatly exaggerated funny stories—like American tall tales—that bring bursts of merriment around the night cooking fires in the village. But it is easier to remember the altogether weary hopeless faces in the fields, the sad voice saying,

"Zeinab's baby was born blind. Did you know?" It is impossible to forget that my people, who by nature are independent, freedom-loving, are really slaves—slaves to hunger, slaves to need.

Sometime the time will come when these villagers will own their own land—even now the government is working toward this—instead of its being owned by an absentee landlord. More of them will have an ox and a donkey living in their

Village musicians. The reward a bowl of fruit.

homes with them, adding warmth to their cottage, hours to their day. Still, the peasants I know are used to a paternal factor in their life. What about the rotation of crops, what about the rebuilding of the land, what about keeping up the kanats? It seems they must trade their dependence upon the landlord and his overseer for dependence on something, or someone else. It seems to me that tenant ownership of the land will not solve the whole problem. And I think of the headman of the Azerbaijan village who said, "So many idle months."

I seem to feel that in this statement I will find the answer to the villagers' problems. When I am wise.

# THERE ARE MANY QUESTIONS

I DO not know when I first went outside myself and looked
inside at my soul. Perhaps it was the evening at my uncle's
home when he said, "Najmeh is not a good Moslem."

I could not believe that he had really said these words. I
could not believe, even if the words had been spoken by my
very good uncle, that they were true. I felt his wife's eyes on
my face, and looking toward her I saw that there was understanding and deep affection on her sweet face, but she did not
say a word to refute my uncle's harsh statement.

We, my mother and I, were guests in her half-brother's
home. Often the two of us spent an evening there; since I had
grown up I could spend fewer and fewer days with this aunt
who loved me. My uncle, who was very rich and very religious,
was also very warm toward my mother and her children. This
evening we had been talking of the pilgrimage to Mecca. In
the Islamic religion every one longs to go one time at least to
the holy city of Mecca. It takes a great deal of money to do
this, not for the traveling alone, but for the alms one must
give on this holy pilgrimage. When my father died my mother
had enough money to give the alms and go to Mecca. How-

ever, she chose to sell her property a parcel at a time to rear her family, to make a home for us, and to educate us.

This evening my uncle was saying that she should have gone to Mecca and I said, more politely than it can be said in English, of course, "Uncle, why do you give alms to the shrines that already have very much money instead of helping the poor of Teheran or the starving people of the villages?"

He looked at me as if I had said a very evil thing. He did not answer the question, just said flatly, "Najmeh is not a good Moslem."

I did not answer. Maybe he was right. But I now had my eyes on something that before had been hidden.

At first I felt anger at my uncle for speaking such words. If I were not a good Moslem, whose fault was it? It was in his home that I had seen people living devotedly according to the ancient customs. It was there that my brother Mosen had learned to join in the call to prayer—"Allah Akbar, Allah Akbar, Allah Akbar." It was his wife who had first taught me the devotions, bribing me to learn them with candy and cookies and fruits. She had taught me the mohbah, the mostahab, the makruh, the haram, and the vajeb.

But now my uncle had said, "Najmeh is not a good Moslem."

Going home I studied his words. I read the Koran every day, most often aloud to my mother, and found in every word enough to live by for many years. I kept the fast of Ramazon. Although I had never been to Mecca I had been to the sacred shrines closer to Teheran. I thought now of the shrine of Imam Riza in Meshed. I remembered going at midnight to pray. A most beautiful voice ringing like a deep gong from the minaret had announced the time for praying—a beautiful voice that shook my soul—and the camels coming under the deep blue sky to bring food for the city. God had been with me in Meshed, though I had never been to Mecca.

I was clean. I prayed before dawn, twice at noon, and again in the evenings, and while I did not give regular alms I was still young and gave of what I had to those I saw in need. I thought of the vajeb, the mohbah, the mostahab, the makruh, and the haram. I could not think of sins which I had committed, only good things that I had left undone, sometimes, perhaps.

It is early morning in Meshed.

"Mother," I said, troubled, "am I a good Moslem?"

"Think nothing of those words," my mother said, and I knew she had been concerned by them, too. "You are an angel. We do not need to go to that home again."

But I knew how much the closeness of her brother had meant to her since the death of my father so I said, "It is all right. He has not broken my feelings."

But I could not forget his words and perhaps they were good for me, because I searched my mind and my heart, and I studied and read more religious books, trying to measure my own soul. This sounds unusual for a young girl, but in my country the religious life is important. For the first time I really saw Mohammed, the prophet, as a young man, wanting to believe, but wondering what to believe.

When Mohammed was an orphaned camel driver, going from Mecca to Syria, or perhaps even Egypt, the religion of Arabia was much as it had been for several thousand years. Each tribe worshiped its own tribal fetishes, rocks and trees and stars, agreeing only on the worship of a black rock in a temple called Kaaba, in the city of Mecca. In those days the Arabians made an annual pilgrimage to Mecca and for three months out of the year all travelers going to the city were safe from robber bands.

But Mohammed—his name was Ubu'l Kassim, then—was not content with a god who was powerful just in one village, or even in Arabia. He had an inquisitive mind, he was a philosopher and a visionary. Everywhere he went his eyes, his mind, and his heart were open. When he was twenty-five he married Khadija, a widow of forty who understood him and appreciated his search for God. Now, no longer dependent upon his own work for his daily bread, he had time to go into the desert and think and pray. It was here that he learned that the only real happiness, the only real peace, comes in submission to God, the one God who is the God of all man. *Islam*, the name of the religion he founded, means submission. It was here that he was appointed, in a vision, to be the prophet of this new religion, of this all-powerful God, to Mecca.

There are those who say that Mohammed brought these ideas out of his own disturbed, uncertain soul; that they did not come to him in a miraculous vision. I believe, with other Moslems, that the searching of his own soul and mind, his eager piecing together of the religious truths he heard in the market places of the world, prepared him for his visions and did not make them unnecessary.

First he told his wife of his visions, and she believed him. She was a perceptive woman, and she believed. Then he told his friends, moving cautiously so as not to anger the priesthood of Kaaba. At last he announced the vision to the world and at once there rose the resistance that seems to have faced all religious truth whenever it has been revealed. Finally, to save his life, he agreed to stop teaching Islam to the Meccans, and taught only strangers in the market places of this world trade center. This was best for the eventual triumph of the religion because every stranger converted carried the message to his own people.

When Mohammed was fifty-two an assassination committee met in Mecca determined to kill him. He fled to Yathrib, now called Medina. With only Abu Bakr, his most trusted disciple, he hid in a cave far out in the desert to the south of Mecca. "Behold we are but two against a whole multitude," Abu Bakr cried. Mohammed answered, "Nay, not two, but three—for God is with us."

This was the *hejira*, or flight; year one in the Moslem calendar. Just ten years after the hejira, Mohammed died, but already Islam had begun to spread over the earth. Already the Koran, a book of sacred revelations, had perhaps been written to guide the thinking and living of millions of his followers down to this day.

After my uncle's words I spent more time than ever with the Koran. The words took on deeper and deeper meaning.

Praise be to God, Lord of the worlds
The compassionate, the merciful
King on the day of reckoning!
Thee only do we worship and to Thee we cry for help.
Guide Thou us on the straight path,
The path of those to whom Thou hast been gracious;
With whom Thou are not angry, and who go not astray.

But there were other things which I had read carelessly before which now began to trouble me. For the first time I began to think of religion as a matter of chance and of geography.

I was born in Persia, in a Moslem home, so I was what the Koran calls a "believer." But I was a believer not because of any special quality in my own heart but because my mother taught me these things. Had I been born in another country perhaps a Christian mother would have led me to a different church telling me different things.

In the Koran I read that all unbelievers are destined to hell; but as I read other books I found that Catholics, for example, believe that the unbaptized go to hell. I was worried. I had said so often in my devotions that God is compassionate and merciful, and it was hard for me to add in my thoughts, "to Moslems, only."

Maybe that is why I am not a "good Moslem." I do not have strongly enough the feeling that we are a special people. I think of the world worshiping God in different ways but God being compassionate to all.

Often, here in America, people ask me if I believe the Koran. Of course I believe the Koran, but I believe—what do you call it?—historically. Besides, I am not wise enough to say I do believe or I don't believe every special thing.

When Mohammed was living, his ideas were of the greatest

and best. He saw around him a great deal of uncleanliness and sin. In the Koran he speaks against these things. Time has changed many things, and maybe some of these laws do not fit today. As I read I am sorry that the Koran speaks about women because the Koranic laws concerning women have kept us inferior for all of these centuries, but in my mind I know that at one time those very same laws elevated the position of women when conditions were different.

Many Christians do not know that Christ is spoken of in the Koran as a great teacher. It is only the elevation of Christ to a position equal with that of God that Mohammed objected to. He had learned from the Jews that there is but one God, God, and he could not believe that God's place can be shared, making two Gods instead of one.

When he heard the Eastern Christians say, "Mary, Mother of God," it troubled him because he felt that no mortal woman could give birth to a God.

And because Christ was spoken of in the Koran, I read of the Christian religion, but it did not appeal to me. More appealing was the ancient worship of Zoroaster or Zarathustra as he is sometimes called. They do not take new members into their worship so I could not be a Parsee even if I wished to, but I read of the religion.

Zoroaster was born more than 600 years B.C. (The B.C. is still difficult for me. I would rather think a hundred years before Buddha and two hundred years before Socrates), and yet his ideas were so good that they make a frame for our thinking today. He believed that there are two great forces, the force of good and the force of evil. Both of these forces I have felt. He believed that these forces were fighting against each other, and I have felt this battle in my own heart.

He believed, too, that man is a creature of dignity and

worth and that he can co-operate with God in overcoming evil; that evil cannot be overcome unless man does work with God. He taught that the dead will live again, that man's soul, in fact, never dies, and that sometime the heavenly Paradise, "the abode of song," will be open for all the souls that are pure.

As I read more and more of the philosophy of Zoroaster, I felt that in the wide frame for religion that it set I could put all I knew of the Islamic Faith and live both faithfully. It is easier to please God by doing specific acts and leaving other acts undone than it is to take up the Banner of God, and co-operate intelligently, deciding at every turn according to the best thought and the conscience. But the latter course is the best for me, I think. I know my duty. My heart knows right from wrong. Maybe I am not a good Moslem. Now I want to be a good person more than I want to be a good Moslem, I think. But I will not tell my uncle.

I had settled the idea for myself, but still it would not remain settled. I thought of the acts that are to be performed according to my religion. They are good acts. Behind each of them there is much for me to live by. Again I was confused.

It was, I think, because I was trying to make religion a matter of the head alone when it should be a matter of the heart. Now I tried to take my head out of the matter and let my heart lead the way. There is much that is mystic in religion. Much that is felt by the reaching soul. We have in the East a philosophy called Sufism which fills our poetry and keeps our spirits climbing toward God. It is a hard thing to explain, this thing that is beyond words, beyond special acts. It is a desire to know God in a way that cannot be expressed in words, to be accepted by God's pure essence of spirit. I cannot say it, you see. Abu Said's words: "What thou hast in thy hand, throw away; what thou hast in thy head (thy ambitions) resign; whatsoever cometh upon thee, turn not back. God is not only almighty and all good, but is the sole source of Being and Beauty, and indeed the One being and the One beauty," are as clear as words can be.

But clearer than words is the symbol—the ritual. In the Moslem Faith the turning toward Mecca, the fasting, the daily devotions—all of these may be empty, done without heart or without mind. But they may be full, done with every hungry part of the body reaching toward the food of faith.

My uncle had said, "Najmeh is not a good Moslem"; yet I knew that I tried to love God, I tried to be clean, to be kind, I decided to ask God to help me.

Once when I was going to Meshed on a holy pilgrimage many asked, "What are you going to ask God for?"

At the shrines of the twelve Imams pilgrims pray, "Oh, Imam—give me this. Give me that." And being in a sacred place makes the prayer seem to ascend rather than to bend back to the earth again after it is spoken. And as they pray they expect an answer because the Imams of my faith were given special divine grace.

And so, many asked me what am I going to ask for at Meshed.

"Why should I say, 'Give me a home, give me a new car, give me travel?' " I ask. "It is my prayer that God should give me a clean heart and a good head so that I can gain the things that are good."

People ask me if I believe in Fate—Kismet.

Suppose you are on board a ship, a very enormous ship. In that ship you may do as you please. You may sleep, wake, eat, bathe, play, walk in the way that you wish to. You may go where you wish to go. But there is one limit to your freedom. If you go too far you are lost in the sea. To me Kismet is like this. There is freedom, liberty, room for initiative; but each of us is placed on a certain ship and the ship we are placed on determines our limits. Maybe I do not explain this clearly.

(In a new language it is easy to say "cat," "dog," "mother," "animal" but it is hard to explain ideas. That is why I must use this symbol.)

When we pray we must ask God to help us to do the things that are our particular destiny.

Once I heard a man, Hadayat, say to his wife, "You pray for the price of sugar and tea to go higher. If it does I'll take you to Meshed."

I was very angry. Sugar and tea, the two things that the poorest man in the city and in the village must buy, and he was holding them for a profit! But this is sometimes religion in my country.

I like these words from the Benidad, a religious book: (Notice how the cattle, the fodder, and the dog come before the wife.) Where is the Ideal Life?

It is where one of the faithful erects a house with a priest within, with cattle, with a wife, with children, and good herds within; and where the cattle continue to thrive, virtue to thrive, fodder to thrive, the dog to thrive, the wife to thrive, the child to thrive, the fire to thrive and every blessing of life to thrive. It is where one of the faithful cultivates most corn, grass and fruit; where he waters ground that is dry, or drains ground that is wet.

## · 13 ·

# I SEE HISTORY MADE

I WAS sixteen and I was going to my first formal function of importance. Each time that the Majlis is called into session there is a reception preceding the opening day. This year the reception was even more important. For the first time I remember the Senate was being called to meet, also.

According to the constitution granted to the people of Iran, there were to be two houses in the parliament as there are in the United States and in England. The house of Majlis met. At first they co-operated with Reza Shah, later they nodded yes to each thing that he asked. They were what you call in America a "rubber stamp" parliament.

But Reza had gone with the disastrous three-day war, and his son was determined to live according to the constitution of a limited monarchy. Now Persia was facing a problem so serious that the whole country must stand together, and the Senate had been called to add its weight to the Persian side of the problem.

At Yalta, when the second front was planned, Persia had been promised that six months after the end of hostilities

Russia and America and Great Britain would leave our country. According to that promise the United States and Great
Britain withdrew but Russia stayed on. Even with Russia worn
out from war, Persia could be no match for so great an expanse
of land, so great a population, so great a fervor as the political
philosophy of the people generated, so great a dictator as
conducted the affairs of Russia.

Our one chance was to put the whole matter before the
Security Council of the United Nations. (Strong nations
like America do not realize what such a council means to
smaller nations.) To prepare for this move the Senate was to
hold its first meeting.

There is, in Teheran, a wide avenue just three blocks long
that is one of the most beautiful streets in the world. We call it
Sadii. It is edged with fine shops—one of these is the book-
store "Speh Salar" where I often asked, "What is the best in
books today?"—and in one intersection there is a beautiful
piece of statuary which holds a great light. Four lions with
their backs to the statuary and their faces pointing to the
corners are symbolic of the glories of Persia. They are the same
lions that appear on our flag. At the end of the street is the
Senate building. At the right of the building is the most
beautiful *masjid* in Teheran, a mosque where many famous
funerals have been held.

The Senate building itself is too beautiful for my words.
I have seen many buildings in America which are, in a way,
copies of it with its dome, its façades. The windows that front
the street are barred; not like jailhouse windows but with great
beauty. There are three entrances. The one on the north end
is flanked by two lions and the turning door is called Mozafer,
meaning, "Now everything is right." This door is for every-

body. Nearly at the center of the building is another door which is reached by a recessed passageway and eight or maybe ten steps. Here, too, is the lion. This entrance is for special people—Senators, Majlis, ambassadors, those of high family. At the south end is a plain doorway for the tradespeople.

On this night of the reception the street was lighted like the middle of the day. Everyone in beautiful dress was moving toward the Senate building. Ashbage, Fahri, and I climbed the steps and entered through the center door. The interior of the building is decorated with exquisite ancient design. If we had had time we could have enjoyed the delicacy and rich color of the design for many hours, but the people were moving toward the garden where the best food was served with tea.

I was excited as different people were pointed out to me. Most important was Ahmad Ghavan Sultaneh, the premier who had on his shoulders the problem of moving Russia from our country and doing much else in rebuilding and building. I would have liked to talk to Ahmad Ghavan Sultaneh but I was a child, a woman.

Instead I spoke to the Senator from Shiraz who had forgotten, I hope, how I had troubled him in the Bastille.

"I would like to see the meeting of the Senate," I told him.

"But of course you can," he said. "In the gallery visitors may watch and listen."

"I will do that," I said. Later Fahri said that she, too, would like to visit the Senate chambers.

"I think you girls will be disappointed," Ashbage said. But he did not say how or why.

The next morning Mother asked, "Did you enjoy the reception? Did you meet Premier Sultaneh?"

"It was exciting," I said. "But Fahri and I want to visit Parliament in session. This was a wonderful party, but just a party."

"It would be good to visit the Senate and the Majlis," my mother said. "I think perhaps we are seeing history made." Then she was quiet, her brown eyes going over my face without seeing it. "I have seen history made, I think. I have seen the people growing in power. I think I remember the Bast. I was a very little girl, but I am sure that I remember it."

Always I had gone to The Match when I wanted to hear a story. Now I realized that my mother had very rich stories of another kind. Not stories of magic, but stories of the waking of my country.

"The Bast!" I said, remembering what I had read of it in the books of history. "Tell me what it was really like to the people."

"It was forty years ago," Mother said, "but it might have been yesterday. Forty years from now when you think of the World War II you will remember how hard it was to get food. You will remember the food we had put away and how we counted it carefully when we ate it. When I remember the Bast, I remember it in the same way. I think first of the bazaars being closed."

Probably Mother, being so young, could not remember Muzaffar-ed-Din Shah who was King at the time of the Bast. She would not have known that he had borrowed money from many foreign powers, using the money for himself and for his harem, and granting to the creditors concessions that enslaved the country.

I knew the rest of the story. How in a few days Muzaffar-ed-Din Shah died by some foul means and how Mohammed Ali

Shah took his place. I knew how the young Shah first granted a constitution then attempted to nullify it and how the Russian government which had successfully put down its own revolution attempted to help him. I coaxed Mother to tell of the rising of the people against their Russian-supported Shah, and of the siege of Teheran by the forces of the people, but she would say little.

When Mohammed Ali Shah was forced to abdicate, his twelve-year-old son, Sultan Ahmed, took the throne. Of Sultan Ahmed Mother had many stories. My father had been at first his teacher, later his adviser. Father had traveled much with Shah Ahmed in Europe. The Shah feared violence. It is not strange because since the time of the Bast there had been nothing but violence in my country, but that his fear of his own death should keep him from doing anything for his people is tragic. Whose life—what man's life—means that much, I wonder. Perhaps he was relieved when Reza Shah who at first feared nothing, no person, no other nation, took over the power in my country.

"I hope," said my mother, "that this meeting of the Senate is the beginning of something good." Then she sighed, "There is so much to be done."

I looked at my mother with surprised eyes. Never had I thought that she was interested in politics. Never had I thought that she had an opinion about these things.

"There are many to do much," I said, feeling very eager to see this Senate in session.

How can I tell you of the meeting of the Senate? After all, Fahri did not go with me. I went, instead, with friends. There in the beautiful room the men, rising, quarreled like little children. They spat rude words at each other—words I scarcely knew in Persian and for which I have no English.

I left sadly. "How can we do much? How can we make the future?" I asked myself. Ashbage had said that I would be disappointed.

My new-found interest in politics sent me to books. I thought it would give me a feeling of assurance, perhaps, to read of the past greatness of my country.

Once the Arabian horse and the camel had a conversation. This is a story that The Match told me. "What a strange creature you are," said the horse to the camel. "What do you do for man?"

"I carry him from place to place," said the camel.

"You?" The horse laughed. "You slow old thing."

"I'll race you to Isfahan," offered the camel.

"Indeed?" said the haughty horse. "Have you seen me run?"

"I have seen you," said the camel.

So the race began. The very quick Arabian horse was soon out of sight and the camel, little by little going along, was not even in the dust of the horse. But he kept on going. At the first oasis the horse was eating grass. "You!" he laughed to the camel; then he trotted away, his head and tail high.

But the camel little by little kept going along.

Finally at the last oasis the camel came upon the horse sleeping. He stepped softly so as not to waken the horse, and passing him, arrived first at Isfahan.

I thought often of this story as I sat in my room reading, reading, reading. I loved history. The story of my country. But my country had been the swift horse. The Western world had been the camel. Once we had been out and away, our heads high. But for many years we had been sleeping. Past us the world went softly so as not to waken us. Now the rest of the world was at Isfahan and we were waking and flexing our muscles, and stretching, at a by-passed oasis.

I loved to read about the ancient kings—the days of the Medes and the Persians, the time when Cyrus the Second threw off the yoke of the Medes and moved to the Mediterranean coast through Lydia and the Greek colony of Ionia; of Cambyses II who conquered Egypt and Darius who moved west as far as the Danube conquering Macedonia and Thrace. Once Persia was a greater empire than Rome ever was. Cyrus and his successors believed in one supreme God who had entrusted them with the task of uniting the people of the earth in one kingdom of justice and peace. On the ruins of the palace of Pasargardae Darius' words still are readable. "A great God is Ahura Mazda, who created the earth, who created heaven, who created man, who created abundance for men, who invested Darius with divine wisdom and virtue."

I had seen the art treasures, the ruins of the palaces of the Achaemenian kings, designed sometimes by Greeks who had been banished from their own country and had taken refuge in ours.

Xerxes was defeated by the Greeks, but soon came Alexander, who is a national hero of ours. Firdausi wrote that Alexander was a grandson of Darius I, because Philip of Macedon was married to Darius' daughter. He loved the Persian life. He married two Persian wives. In most ways he was exactly Persian. Many what you call "legends" are told of him in my country.

Then there was a line of Sassanian kings. You know Haroun-al-Rashid of the Sassanian kings because he is the king of the *Arabian Nights* stories. And there was the Safavid dynasty, kings who were real descendants of the martyr, Ali.

I like best the stories of Shah Abbas who lived at the

same time as the English Queen Elizabeth. Meeting his name in my reading is like coming upon a very good friend. Many times The Match has told stories about this man.

Shah Abbas, The Match said, was a magic King. He loved his people and never could sleep until all of the people were fed. Each night, dressed in common clothes, he walked through the streets of his city asking people if they were happy. In his hand he carried a *kishkule*—sort of an oval shaped dish with a handle—filled with food for those in need.

One night as he was walking the street he heard the singing of a girl coming from a little hut. He entered and saw that the girl was blind and that the man who played the lyre for her was a simple man.

"May I come in? I have some food. Share and we'll eat together."

"Come in," said the man, not recognizing the Shah.

"What do you do to earn your bread?" Shah Abbas asked after they had eaten together.

"I sit upon the street and mend the shoes of the people passing by," he answered.

"What would you do if the Shah made a law against repairing shoes?"

The shoemaker laughed. "Shah Abbas would not do that. He is kind."

The next morning early Shah Abbas made that law. The next evening he passed the little hut. More music was coming out into the street. "May I come in? I have food. Share and we'll eat together."

And so they ate together again and Shah Abbas asked, "What did you do today?"

"Today I did very well. The King would not allow me to

mend shoes so I emptied water for the people. Emptying water is better than mending shoes. I have more money tonight."

"What would you do if Shah Abbas made an edict against the emptying of the water?" the Shah asked.

"He is a kind man. He will not do that."

But the next morning Shah Abbas announced that no man should empty water for a week. And that night he went again to the hut. "What did you do today?" he asked, interrupting the merrymaking.

"The King will not let me empty water so I emptied the garbage. Emptying the garbage is better than emptying the water."

"What would you do if the King—?"

The man looked at Shah Abbas. "I think you are an evil man," he said. "Every time what you say comes true."

The next morning Shah Abbas had the man brought to the palace. He had him dressed in beautiful clothing and gave him a sword to hold all the day. That way he was sure that he could not work.

That night as the Shah walked through the streets there was very much music coming from the hut. "What did you do today?" he asked the man.

"Today? I could not work. But today I sold a fine sword and got in its place a sword of wood."

The next morning Shah Abbas, dressed in red because it was the day for the executions, called the man before the throne. "Today you are the executioner," he said. "I will have the man that must die brought to you and with your sword you must kill him."

Now, poor man. He did not know that the King was the stranger who had been in his home, but he did know his sword was of wood and Shah Abbas would find him out. He must think very fast. He put his hand on the sword and prayed very loud. "Allah," he cried, "if this man is truly guilty let my sword cut off his head. If this man is innocent let my sword turn to wood."

When he drew the sword it was of wood.

Shah Abbas laughed. "You are ambitious. You are clever. I will reward you."

And I think when I remember The Match's story of Shah Abbas that perhaps this story is not about the Shah at all but about my people. I think with people like this, clever, ambitious, people with initiative, surely we shall really waken and save ourselves.

Our trouble is that we have not been prepared to use our ambition and our cleverness for our country. Where few people read and write, the newspaper is not a real force in national life. There is the radio, but it is not owned by the common people but by those who could use the newspaper. For getting news there is the bathhouse and the bazaar and in both of these places rumors grow away from the fact and the fact is lost.

One day in America I saw a six-year-old child bring home a certificate for special service. That little girl with three front teeth missing, had been a member of the school council, discussing the problems of the children at the school and helping to make the laws to answer the problems. In Persia there is nothing like this. We must know how to use power rather than crying for it, then throwing it away.

It is no wonder that Reza Shah disregarded the people.

At his first coming he had a dream—a dream of modernization, and of growth, that only unselfish service and real patriotism could bring to life. It was no wonder that he grew impatient with people and worked alone toward that dream.

And thinking of Reza Shah I realized that during my own lifetime most of the modern history of Persia has been made.

I was not born when Reza became prime minister, when in 1921 he became Shah; but with my own memory, I can recall most of the happenings of Reza Shah's rule. I remember Fahri, hanging back and insisting that she could not leave the house without the veil when Reza Shah abolished the veil. I still go to the home of the wife of my uncle in daylight because she will not leave her house except in the dark of night since she is very religious and cannot go without the veil. Her heart will not let her. I have seen carriages and cars stopped by the police because the women in them were veiled.

Once at Meshed I met the two very handsome sons of Premier Teymourtache who was the chief collaborator and councilor of Reza Shah. Everyone knew that Teymourtache grew wealthy getting concessions for certain people from Reza for a mudakhil (this is what the receiver called a sum of money that was given him for such a special service. The giver calls it a pishkesh—that which leads or comes before).

I had heard it said in my country, too, that if you want something from Teymourtache send the beautiful wife. The beautiful wife goes one night to Teymourtache and the next day the husband is elevated in office. This is bathhouse talk. I do not know this for a fact. But my people have many stories about such wives. This story The Match did not tell me.

Once there were two men who were friends. Bab had a very beautiful wife. Ali had a very ugly wife who had borne him seven children and was good at keeping the house.

"Bab," Ali asked, "how do you know that your wife is true to you?"

"Why, that's silly. Of course she is true to me."

"I do not think so. Let us test her."

"She is true to me. No need to test."

"I will give you much silver if I am wrong, but I think she is not true."

"Much silver! We will test her. How do we do this?"

"It is easy," Ali said. "When she is in bed tonight you say, 'The evil one will lay hold of your foot if you tell a lie.' After you will say, 'Do you love me? Have you always been true to me?' Then I will lay hold of her feet."

"It is a bargain," Bab agreed.

So that night he hid Ali at the foot of his bed. He said just as Ali had told him, "My dear, do you love me? Are you exactly true to me?"

"Why, of course, silly. How can you ask?"

Then Ali laid hold of her feet. "I will tell the truth," she cried. "You know the necklace that I told you my mother gave me. It was from a lover."

Again Ali pinched her ankle. "And that bracelet I said was from my sister. It is from another lover."

"You see, Bab," Ali said the next day. "Your wife is untrue. You must give me the silver."

"First let us test your wife. Let us see that she is true. I do not believe it."

"My so ugly wife! Of course she is true. How could she be untrue with a face like hers?"

But that night Bab was hidden at the foot of Ali's bed and when Ali asked, "Dear, do you love me? Are you faithful to me alone?" she said, "How silly. Who would want me?"

Bab laid hold of her ankle and she cried, "I am telling. Devil, let me go. Let me go. I am telling. Do you know that man who comes to clean? I gave him your coat and he took me. And do you know the garbage man who empties our waste? I gave him a small prayer carpet and he took me."

The next day when Ali and Bab met they could not decide who should give the silver and who should receive it. At last Bab said, "But of course I am the winner. Your woman gives something of your possessions; mine brings something into the home."

Perhaps this is more than a story. Perhaps, as they say at the bathhouse, a beautiful wife could win office for her husband more easily than he could win it through faithfulness and intelligent service.

At school I had a girl friend who was much in love with a handsome young man. She never told the young man. She was too shy. At the same time Teymourtache was very interested in an attractive, but not beautiful woman. When my friend found that the young man she loved had become the lover of this friend of Teymourtache, she took her own life.

So I knew of Teymourtache and paid special attention when he and Reza Shah came to a parting. Teymourtache was put in prison and there he died either from strangling or from poison. Nobody ever knew.

This was an often-repeated pattern of violence in my country. It is the pattern wherever one man holds others by fear, because he, too, must fear.

When I was in Rome I thought of Nero. I might have thought of Virgil or of Cicero, but I thought of Nero. I thought of all the ancient people who had the beautiful idea that Nero could not understand. And I thought of how sometimes violence builds a dream as it sometimes has in my country when some dictator gets a vision of a good future and pushes toward that future through bloodshed and violence.

A dancing girl. Not too nice, perhaps.

And of how sometimes violence tries to choke a dream. Seeing Rome I knew that violence can never really do that. Old Rome falling to ruins and the Christian philosophy growing bigger and brighter with time going on.

Reza Shah had this fine patriotic dream and to bring it to life he used the tools at his hand. To me that is the great danger of long terms of office. One does not learn to depend upon willing co-operation. I like the American system of reconsidering the head of the country every four years. When one man holds office for a long time his dream obsesses him. In everybody he sees a potential thief of his power, a wrecker of his plans. Such people must be erased. There must be violence.

All my life I heard talk of the army. In my country the army may be turned against an outside enemy or against the people themselves. I think you have nothing in America to help you to understand the situation of the tribes of Persia. In America individual freedom is important. In Persia individual freedom is important but even more important is tribal freedom.

If an American traveling in a distant country is asked who he is he will say, "I'm an American," not, "I'm a Yankee." If a man from my country were asked, he might say, "I'm a Kurd," or "I am a Shirazian."

Each region has developed its own personality. Just as you have jokes about the Jews and the Irish, the people of my country criticize each other in humor. The Shirazian woman is supposed to be an attractive witch. She is cartooned as saying to one from Teheran, "Been married a week. Still you have your husband?" Of the Kazvanian it is said, "He has money because he never eats." A man from Isfahan asks a man from another district, "What makes you so smart?" The answer is, "Last night I slept in Isfahan!"

Too, there are great traditions centering around each of these tribes. Saladin was a Kurd, for example. Tribesmen are willing to lose their lives rather than be absorbed.

When Reza Shah first came to power he used the army to

conquer these tribes. I do not remember this, I think, but I am acquainted with it in a roundabout way. When he had conquered a tribe he invited its chieftain to come to Teheran. Some came rather willingly, some came as prisoners and were held as hostages. The rebellious ones hated the city but the others lived in a lazy ease they had never known and their sons and daughters were many of them known to my brothers and me.

And the army itself? Always I had been interested in the village, and in every village there was sorrow over conscription. I have never known the time when the villagers did not consider conscription a burden too heavy to carry.

Now that I was older I could look back on our three-day war with the British and the Russians, three days when we hoped desperately that the Germans would come, as just an incident in the long subjugation of my people. I knew that there were outside reasons why Reza Shah had been so successful in building the modernization of my country. Russia, after the close of the World War I, had been busy first with her five-year plan then with her fifteen-year plan. She had had to do for herself what Reza had been trying to do for Persia. We had quarreled across the border, we had argued about fishing in the Caspian Sea, but I think the great bear felt that any time he put out his paw he could drag Persia into his body. Britain, operating our oil fields for gain, had been pleased to keep us a sovereign state. It served her purpose. But she felt that at any time it would be easy to push up from the gulf and take what she wanted from us.

And in the three-day war they both showed that they were right. I determined that sometime I would see England, thinking again, Who is this country, so small on the map, that it can squeeze the world in its hand?

I was sixteen and America had left Persia and Great Britain had left Persia but Russia was still there. That can be seen by the activities of the Democratic Party in Azerbaijan. The leader of this rebellious party was Pisheveri. With him I had a very roundabout acquaintance. Once when I had been traveling in the south with three kinsfolk we had stayed in the home of a village woman who had one son and one daughter. The daughter-in-law I remember particularly. She was a Russian girl who had fled the Communist regime into Persia. She had married a Persian boy who one month after his marriage was taken a political prisoner. She lived on with her mother-in-law rearing a son who had never seen his father. She did all the work of a man. While we were there she, with her strong masculine hands, killed a sheep and dressed it. I cannot forget such a woman!

The daughter was not at home. She was the wife of Pisheveri and lived in Azerbaijan. Between the end of the war and 1946 we heard often of this Pisheveri. He was to Azerbaijan what you call—Quisling. With the help of Russia he became very important.

One time much later I saw this Russian sheep-killing woman on the street in Teheran. "Hello," I said, when she spoke to me, but I wondered who she was. She looked so sad, so sick. "How are you?" I asked with real desire for an answer when I recognized who she was.

"I am not well," she said. Then she cried as she told me that when the Russians left, Pisheveri was so hated by his neighbors that he had to flee into Russia. With him went his wife, the mother-in-law, the husband of this girl who had been released from prison after the abdication of Reza, even her son. She cannot, of course, return to Russia and so she is alone.

Much of modern Persia's history was in my memory. I had seen the waking of the horse in the story of The Match. Premier Sultaneh would put the problem of the expulsion of Russia before the Security Council of the United Nations. At sixteen I felt that a new period was opening for my country. I felt the waking horse would again be swift and strong and reach Isfahan not too far behind the camel.

# · 14 ·

# THE SHOP

I HAD spent enough time in dreaming. There were things to be done. I have never been interested in money. Money going and coming. But now I realized that without money I could do nothing for my country.

One Christmas time I walked one block on Pasadena's main street, and I saw just one beggar. He was a blind man, playing a violin and beside him a woman walked, guiding him and holding the cup for coins. Perhaps he was not really a beggar in his own mind. Perhaps he thought he was making something for the pleasure of the people and that he earned the silver that dropped into his cup. There was the familiar ringing of the bell by Salvation Army people, but they are not begging for themselves so that is different.

If I walk one block in Teheran I meet one hundred beggars. They are hungry, cold, discouraged people, who would not, I think, beg if they could do anything else. How is it that other people—people of the West—have learned to provide work for everybody, I wonder. I must travel and find out. And for traveling I must have money.

There is one thing that I could do. I could sew and design and I had ideas. I had finished the design school with the top grades in my class, and there were many things that I knew that are not taught at the school.

Quietly, little by little, I began to plan to open a shop in Teheran. For four or five months I worked. First I sewed many beautiful things by hand. In the dowry of the bride there must be brassieres, slips, nightgowns, many beautiful things that it is traditional to have made by hand. Another custom in my country is for the bride's mother to furnish an entire layette for the first baby that is coming. These things should be sewed by hand, too. Dainty little seams, little tucks, delicate lace, tiny handmade flowers of pastel ribbon.

These are things that take time to make so I sat in my room hour after hour with my needle, singing because I was at last doing something.

When I had finished the things by hand, I bought very beautiful fabric and made ten dresses for display. Then, whenever I saw jewelry that was just right for these dresses I bought that, too, for display. It is an exciting thing to hunt for jewelry in the bazaars. Buying in the bazaars is a game every Persian woman enjoys.

"Beautiful, beautiful!" the seller says, holding an enameled necklace so that the light from the overhead opening will be reflected from each minute speck of color in the design. "Beautiful!" Then he moves his hand just a little so that the light dances from the surface. "For you exactly."

"Not for me," I say. "I think not for me."

"Exactly for you. Your hair, your shining eyes, Lady. Exactly for you."

"I have seen many prettier necklaces."

"Sorry, Lady, pardon so much, but there are no more beautiful necklaces in this world. For a beautiful woman to wear this necklace I would give much. Lady, honor me please. Wear this necklace."

It sounds like he is giving it to me but I know he is not, so I wait.

"For you alone, I make this necklace one hundred dollars."

"One hundred dollars!" I cannot believe my ears. Surely he must have spoken wrong. "For that necklace one hundred dollars! It is not worth twenty."

Now the seller looks very dismayed. "The necklace is so exquisite, so gorgeous, so—"

(You think that the men who write the advertisements for the Hollywood movies have a fine vocabulary but it is not to be compared with the words of praise that are spoken by the sellers in our bazaars.)

"It is not a bad necklace," I say grudgingly.

"Lady, it is the perfect necklace. For you, for you alone I make this necklace ninety-five dollars." He places it on a piece of black cloth and bends far backward to examine it from that distance.

And so I offer twenty-five. Finally the necklace is sold to me for forty dollars. I walk away wondering if I might not have bought it for thirty-five.

If the jewelry is of gold or of silver it is weighed in a scale with the jewelry on one side and a balance on the other like your apothecary scales. The cost is by weight plus the value placed on the workmanship. We do not have junk jewelry in my country.

Now, by myself and without telling anyone of my plans, I began to look for a place to open my shop. I told no one

about the shop because maybe I had a little fear that something might go wrong. One day, I found the perfect place.
There was a new business building going up on a corner not
too far from my home. It would be the exactly right location.

I had not met the businessmen before but now I must. I
arranged to rent a space for my shop. If I would start to pay
rent right then they would let me decorate the shop to suit
myself.

In my mind I could see the shop exactly as I wanted it. I
could see every table, every drapery. I asked for two side walls
and I would design the front and back.

The shop arranged for, I told others of the shop. I needed
money. I had to pay one thousand dollars in advance for the
shop. I needed to buy materials for the decoration, I had to
pay rent and for labor. Of course I turned to my family. At
first they were horrified. "You are just a baby!" I do not know
how many times I heard these words; but my sisters loaned
me the money I needed. It might have disturbed me to see
how sure they were that my shop would fail, but it did not.
I, myself, knew that I could be successful.

One evening Amir came to my home. With him was his
friend Mohammet. When they heard my plans for the shop,
Mohammet studied me with his intelligent deep brown eyes
before he said seriously, "I know you can do it, Najmeh."
When I saw that he really believed in me, my heart made a
special place for this man.

There were many things I had in my home that I could
use in my shop. I had a new sewing machine and an old one.
I had a table, some chairs, a mirror—many things. But there
were things I must buy, too. Half the shop was to be for display and for selling, the other half for working. In the work

room I needed many chairs and several tables. These I hunted for and bought second hand. I hired a man to take off the old paint and to make them clean and shining.

I had a carpenter working for me to make the special display cases and other things that I needed. Those men! Tell them to come at six in the morning and they arrived at eleven. Tell them what to do and they stood giving advice, advice, advice. My idea is never to take advice. If you know your dreams and your duty, no one else can know what is right for you as well as you do. I think they gave advice because they

Salon of the Flower.

did not want to take it. I told and I told how I wanted things. How could I explain? Oh, kill me, I think, I'll never try to open a shop again. I think each one of those old men has taken ten years of my life.

But when the shop was ready it was beautiful. The whole thing was done in shining, shining white, except for four green satin arm chairs and some satin ottomans grouped about a table and a desk. The draperies, hung on very slender silver rods, were of purple, and for the opening I made by hand hundreds of flowers from palest lavender into deep purple. On one table, for example, there was a tall silver vase with a purple flower. At the base of the vase there was a bag, a handkerchief, a pair of long, slender gloves. It was beautiful. In the window I had a very small, very beautiful display. In the salon there was a bright new radio and a bright new sewing machine. Everything was new and clean and very delicate. In the sewing room the chairs and tables were at last refinished and shining, too. There were good sewing machines, and a samovar for heating water so that the girls who sewed for me could make tea and other things for their lunch.

Just before the opening I employed two women who had been making dresses in their homes. They were excellent seamstresses and were pleased with regular employment. On the same day as I employed the women, I sent out letters to my friends and Fahri's and Fahti's telling about the shop and inviting them to the opening.

There was just one more thing that I needed. I needed a dependable person to keep the shop clean, to run errands, to deliver dresses, to sleep in the shop at night and in the winter keep the fires going. My sister Fahti knew just the person. Fahti had now moved to Teheran and with her family servants had come a seventeen-year-old boy, Ishmael, whom she no longer needed.

I talked with Ishmael and explained my needs. He was a bright boy. It would be a good thing to have a young man who would do as I said, not an old man pouring out advice. I employed him and bought him new clothing as his country-made clothes would be unsuitable with my shop. He was proud of those clothes! Probably the first new clothes he had ever had and he was almost eighteen.

I do not remember a single thing about the first day. So many people coming and going! So many people looking at the fashion books on the table. So many asking about where to buy suitable materials, and making reservations for interviews and fittings. The whisper about my shop that I started by writing notes to my friends and the friends of Fahri and Fahti became a great wind blowing. Everybody was coming.

Perhaps it is because until so recently women wore only styleless, ancient clothes that women now take such an interest in fashion. Maybe it is because so many of them lead almost empty lives and purchasing clothes is recreation. But I think the real reason is that American and French moving pictures have given the women of my country a great desire to dress in the Western way.

To them Hollywood is the magic word. Just speaking it brings up visions of all that is desirable. And I was like the rest. I had the idea that all Americans live in elegance and luxury and that the moving pictures are photographed in the homes of average people, perhaps.

When I first came to Los Angeles I asked a taxi driver to take me from the Ambassador Hotel in Los Angeles to the corner of Hollywood and Vine. I could hardly hold my heart inside me as we drove through the running bustle of the streets of Los Angeles. How, I wondered, will this end and smooth, sleek Hollywood begin?

The taxi driver stopped his car, jumped out, and opened the door for me. I did not move except maybe my mouth fell open. "Hollywood and Vine," he said.

I got out and let him choose his fare from a handful of coins. I had learned about American money but I couldn't count money in this moment of being shaken out of a beautiful dream.

Hollywood and Vine was like all the city street corners in all the world. I could not believe it. I thought the taxi driver had stupidly put me out someplace else. But I could see the signs. I compared them with the printed name in my book of places I must see. The taxi driver was right and I was stupid. But where were all the beautifully dressed people that the women of Persia admire so in the Hollywood films? Where were the long lines of people elegantly sipping orange juice?

I walked down the street a little way and there I saw bare-footed girls in so scant bathing suits. They were carrying signs. I took my dictionary from my bag. "This place is unfair to organized labor." So this was not an American bathing beauty contest after all, though it looked like the one photographed in Miami except that the signs were on sticks instead of across the breasts of the undressed girls.

I watched the people going by. There was a man in what looked like blue jeans and a fiercely orange shirt of silk and a great hat. I looked around for the horse; but beside him was a woman in a suit so beautiful that I decided to remember the details and make one like it for myself.

I saw a woman with heels two inches tall who wore slacks tight like peeling of fruit around the hips and stomach. In my country a skirt would be worn over such pantaloons. She wore a short jacket of very beautiful fur and carried an evening bag.

When I opened my shop it was a good thing for me that my customers had not stopped at Hollywood and Vine!

Everything from my shop was the best. For an evening dress or dinner dress, maybe one hundred and seventy-five or two hundred dollars. The dresses were designed specially for each individual, cut exactly to fit and finished by hand.

Almost at once I needed more help in the sewing room.

Help was easy to get. Every hour somebody was asking, "Please employ me," and I selecting the best. One day a very good man came to my shop. "Please employ my daughter," he begged. "I have many children and this daughter is good with the needle." I took the girl and gave her special attention.

Now began a new life for me. I was in the shop early in the morning. At nine at night I called a taxi to take me home. During the day I gave myself not a minute to rest. I must talk to businessmen. I must shop for things I needed. I must supervise the sewing. I, myself, must do the designing and cutting.

I was very busy wondering how to be less busy and still get things done when Ishmael came to me. "My lady," he asked shyly, "will you teach me how to write?" So whenever I had a minute I worked with Ishmael on his writing and his reading.

The one thing that drove me most wild about Ishmael was the way he loved to eat. I imagine that he had never had enough to eat; now that he had his wages by the week he constantly bought great sheets of bread. No matter who came into the shop there would be Ishmael, propped against a show case, chewing on one of these magnificent pieces of bread.

He had other little habits, too, that bothered me. One was that he loved the radio. When I got to the shop in the morning there was Ishmael, all tousled of head from recent rising, chewing on bread and listening to the radio while the shop remained uncleaned. "You will have to do better than this or I'll find another," I scolded him.

He looked at me with such sorrowful eyes as he said, "I will, my lady. You can believe me that I will."

Of course I let him stay.

The girls in the shop were a happy group. They ate together at noon and often in the afternoon I'd go in and tell them a story—always with a good meaning—or just talk to them. They were girls from lower-class homes; good, intelligent, willing girls, but without the advantage of education or of fine breeding.

"Never marry a rich man," I told them one afternoon.

"Why not?"

Ishmael with his magnificent bread.

"Why do you want to marry money? So you can buy the beautiful dress, the jewels, the perfume. With these you want to charm the young man. But then, if you are already married— Marrying the old man is like putting the arm all the way around the head in order to feed the mouth. It is better to feed the mouth from the front."

I had a bulletin board and each day I put up a drawing of somebody in the shop. One day I drew a boy with a round pleasant face, eyebrows that met over the nose and winged up at the ends and a great, smiling mouth. In one hand I put a very great sheet of bread. There was much laughter in the shop and Ishmael laughed, too. When he was on an errand to match

some thread, one of the girls said, "There is one way to cut
the appetite for food. That is to have an appetite for love."

There was much laughter and many guesses when after a
little Ishmael's appetite was cut. "Who is he falling in love
with?" the girls wondered.

One Friday Ishmael started out to an Imamzadeh, a local
shrine, for worship. He was wearing his new clothes and he
had in his pocket his week's pay—five dollars. Standing on
the street were two men, their shoulders close together, looking furtively to the right and left. Said one in a Shirazi accent,
"I have this very expensive jewelry and I must get some money
for it. This is a strange city to me and I don't know where to
turn."

With a thumb he rolled back some cotton that covered a
mass of jewels.

Ishmael's eyes grew round.

"I am a stranger here myself," the other man said. "Perhaps
you should ask this gentleman here."

Ishmael was flattered. He told the owner of the jewels that
Teheran has one street, Esamblo, famous for its jewelry. It
was there one should go to exchange his jewels for money,
except that on Friday everything was closed. Tomorrow—

"Even now my wife waits in the station." The man shook
his head sadly. "You wouldn't care to buy these jewels?" he
asked Ishmael.

Ishmael had great dreams of the value of the jewels. He
nearly choked in his eagerness. "I have five dollars," he said.

"Five dollars." The man was scornful.

Now Ishmael could see nothing but the jewels. "You could
have my coat, too." That very new coat that matched the
shop!

"If it weren't that I am a stranger," the man said. But he took Ishmael's week's salary and the coat and reluctantly gave him the jewels. Ishmael ran all the way to Fahti's home, afraid that the man would change his mind. He started a breathless account of the incident, but Fahti said, "Go show your lady."

Then he came to me, his round eyes shining, his face like the sun. "Take them to my mother for safekeeping," I said, and when he returned I talked with him.

"Do you think you gave a fair price for those jewels?" I asked.

He shook his head. "No, my lady, but I can sell them for so very much!"

"You think you cheated the man?"

He nodded, his eyes turned sorrowful, "I am sorry," he said.

"Then it will make you happy to know that you did not cheat him. The jewels are hardly worth one dime."

His face went black. I could see that he would rather have the sin of cheating a stranger on his head than to have lost the week's salary.

I did not need to tell him that since he would cheat other people it was right for him to be cheated.

Time went along and my shop was in Teheran what you call "a rage." Like a fire the popularity grew. Soon I had two men tailors making coats and maybe twenty girls and women busy sewing. Six months and I had paid my sisters what they had loaned me. And I did nothing but work. When I drooped into our home at night my mother would put her arms around me and say, "Baby, I'm proud of you, but you are killing yourself!"

And then came New Year's and all our rush had been like

a spring compared with a fountain. Now when people came into the shop I had time for only "Hello, how are you?" Other girls, now trained, must do some of the fitting. More and more I was having business with men important in industry. They brought fine fabrics as gifts. If I would use these fabrics for my models, many women would be asking where it was bought and who made it. Men gave me jewelry for display. I was sending orders to France for perfume, French jewelry, gloves, things that could be better made in Persia if Persia were really industrialized.

Every day much money came in. I thrust it into the drawer and waited until evening for the counting. One evening when I counted the money there was fifty dollars missing. In a strange flash of memory I saw one girl standing at the desk. At the time, I suppose, I had wondered what she was doing there instead of being in the workroom. I knew that she had taken the fifty dollars. I could hear her father saying, "I have so large a family and she is clever with the needle."

That night I had a taxi take me to her home on an ugly squalid street. It was filled to overcrowding with children of many ages. She came to me with a sick, yellow-white face and when I spoke of the fifty dollars she drew it from the bosom of her dress and gave it to me.

"You may work in my shop until New Year's," I said.

"Until New Year's," she repeated. I had had the taxi driver wait so I got into the car and drove away.

I hate myself for that night. I should not have done what I did. I had to tell her that I could not keep her in the shop if I did not trust her. But I should have given her a chance to try again. And I should not have taken back the fifty dollars. I know now how the desire for that money had grown in her heart like a spreading cancer. I know the suffering that shook her body while she waited a chance to reach that temptation drawer. How can one be hungry, hungry, every day hungry without reaching for food? I was wrong. May God forgive me.

Already I had asked all who worked in the shop what they wanted for a New Year's present. I meant to give a nice gift to every person but I wanted the gift to be something that was needed. Many of the girls asked for a dress, some said a blouse, one said perfume. But Ishmael would not say. He would only look at me with solemn eyes that looked strange under his upwinging brows and say that what he wanted nobody could give him.

"I will buy him a fine watch so that he can rise in time to clean the shop," I told the girls and they laughed and said that would be a good idea.

I had the New Year party at my home, the table heavy with the seven foods that begin with S and much else besides. As each girl entered I gave her a gift and she kissed me on the cheek. When Ishmael came I gave the gift of the watch. "I do not want this watch," he said. "All I want, my lady, is to kiss your hand."

I acted as if I did not understand the special meaning. But all the same I knew why he had eaten less bread. "On New Year's that is your duty," I said. "Kiss the hand and take the watch, too."

I am glad that I was not as stupid and wrong with Ishmael as I was with the fifty-dollar girl. I know that the heart is neither a master nor a servant. Every heart must be respected. When my sisters made a joke of this I was unhappy. And because I was still a little girl in many ways I took a little girl's way of helping Ishmael.

I wrote a note and left it on one of the tables. There was no signature on the note that said, "Why don't you look my way once in a while? I think you are a very handsome person."

After the girls had gone and Ishmael was cleaning up, he found the note and read it. The next day I could see him studying the girls, trying to decide which one it was that thought him a very handsome person. He was happy again, his eyes round and interested under the wing of his eyebrows.

For some time a young girl had been asking for work in the shop. I had seen her very beautiful handwork and had said, "Come back next week." The next week she had come and the next, but every place at the table was occupied. The fourth time she came back I had a place for her and employed her.

She was a very excellent worker, always careful, always fast, always busy. Each day she went out for lunch and I worried about her because I did not know where she was going. I knew that her home was an hour's bus trip from the shop. One day I asked her, "Why aren't you eating in the shop?"

She didn't have an answer at once.

"There is electricity there to make tea and I furnish the tea and the sugar for the girls," I said.

The next day she again went out.

Again I asked her, "Don't you like to take lunch in the shop?" I wondered if she was not well accepted by the girls and felt shy so I said, "Tomorrow eat your lunch with me."

The next day I made tea for the two of us and the girl opened her lunch. Not a sandwich, just one piece of heavy bread. I looked down at the freshly prepared dinner which Ishmael had just brought me from my home. Fruits, rice, barbecued lamb, olives. And I wondered, *What is the differ-*

ence between me and this girl? She is as young as I am. She is very pretty. She is skillful in her work. And she is proud. If each of us had been placed in the other's family what would I be doing?

I was learning. The shop had not made me proud, but humble. I was nothing; opportunity made me something. And I was back to the same, the very same idea. There must be opportunity for everybody in my country. How could this girl keep herself right and good? What had she been doing for life during the weeks that I said, "Come back next week"?

Life was interesting in the shop. I talked with the girls when I had time. I laughed with them. One day when they wasted much time with yak-yak I came back from a business errand with a great deal of chewing gum. "You cannot chew and talk at the same time," I said. There was always a good spirit in the back room. The women and girls were so happy to be employed, so grateful to be working, so appreciative of the feeling of equality in the shop though I was called "My lady."

Once when I was visiting in Shiraz a woman who heard that I was from Teheran asked me if I had visited this new and very fashionable shop, The Flower.

"Yes," I replied, listening very hard.

"I was there when I was in Teheran. It is a very nice place. But that young snip that runs it is so proud!"

In Shiraz I had found a very excellent mirror.

But I could not be friendly with my customers. There were so many going and coming. They were so different. I learned to tell very soon a great deal about them.

The fashion books which were arranged on my table were

French books. You know how the French pictures are: two
or three lines to make a very slender, very tall girl. Many
women who sat on the green satin chairs and gazed with
interest at the pictures in the book were fat and short. In
Persia a double chin and a great abdomen are equivalent to
a mink coat in America: they are a mark of wealth.

"This is the dress for me," said one woman, pointing with
the end of an elegant finger at a so slim model. "First you
should try the surgery," I thought, looking her over with
a polite eye. If only all my customers were like my beautiful
tall sister Fahri. Or if I could make dresses for the young,
slender girls in my shop.

Sometimes I did make dresses for such girls. The Koran
demands a single standard of morals; that is, though men may
have as many as four wives, to those wives they must be
exactly true. But many men have forgotten the Koran. They
came into the shop with pretty young, simple girls, or with
girls who had until recently been pretty and simple.

If a Persian girl makes one mistake she cannot ever live
above it. And what is a mistake? Even to talk to a man in a
public garden, to walk arm in arm down the avenue, to go
on an afternoon excursion. These are mistakes. The only life
open to her is the life of prostitution. She becomes, if she
has culture and charm, the courtesan of one of the wealthy
men and rides in a Cadillac behind polite but contemptuous
drivers. Such girls came into my shop and ordered dresses,
and gowns, and lingerie, and I knew that they were not happy.

Many foreign people had dresses made in the shop. All my
life I had known foreign people. They had been entertained in
my home and friendships close and warm had grown up:
people from Pakistan, Afghanistan, Turkey, Iraq, Arabia,

India, Syria, Egypt. But I had known few Western people.
My sister Fahri had had a close friend, a girl from Czecho-
slovakia married to a friend of Ashbage. To me, until I opened
the shop, she was all European women. Now it was different.
There were many English women whose husbands were connected with the Anglo-Iranian oil operations; there were even
American women, and French.

I did not like the loud voices of the English and American
women, the dull drop, like lead, of the voice at the end of
each sentence, the exaggerated inflection, the wide range of
pitch of their voices. I liked the Persian voice, soft, with an
upward lift at the end of sentences.

But I served all of the women. There was money coming in
to give me a fund for some important project. There was much
that I was learning day by day about the situation of my own
country, about the situation of women in my country.

# I FIND MY MIND

YOU can find anything in the bazaar if you search long enough," people say; and that is almost true. You cannot find a hoe, a rake, a small metal hand tool. The importers of my country are far more interested in bringing in Western cars and great machines, while the fellahs still use the wooden plough, the iron-tipped stick, for their work in the fields. But you can buy perfume, lipstick, fabrics from the very coarse to the very fine, jewelry, art objects of unbelievable beauty, all necessities for the home. The bazaar is like the super drugstore in America, only charming.

It was in a bazaar that I found my own mind. It is strange, but it is true.

There is nothing in America like the bazaars of my country. They are long corridors lighted only by the skylight in each domed ceiling. Sometimes, in the poor bazaars these skylights are just openings, but in the rich bazaars they are made of glass set in lead in intricate and beautiful design. When you enter the arched opening at one end, the corridor stretches, eternal, endless, to a dollar-sized arch at the opposite end.

There are displays of goods on each side of the corridor and behind these displays are store rooms which are usually entered only by the seller. If the customer wants something that is not displayed the seller will go back into the depths of his store room and bring out other goods for display.

In the bazaar there is always the sound of voices. The buyer's voice never really complimentary, sometimes very critical of the goods. Many women shop all day without ever buying. The sellers know this but still they must try. First the seller's voice is very polite, very gracious; then it grows coaxing and finally it is insulting.

"Dear, I am sorry this does not please you. It is the best. With your taste, dear, certainly you realize that! It is wonderful, gorgeous, beautiful!"

"Too expensive. No. Careless workmanship. Dirty color!"

And so it goes until finally the seller turning from a polite merchant into a very tired man screams, "You never buy. Why do you come to bazaar? You have not money!"

This buying and selling is the great national sport in Persia.

I love to see the beautiful things in the bazaar but I do not really enjoy shopping. Men sell everything. If you wish to buy a brassiere or panties you must buy them from a man. To stand in the bazaar while he holds them explaining their value makes me uncomfortable.

For the buying of food there is a little shop on nearly every street, but the real marketing is done at the great open-air morning market. All night the farmers bring in their fruit and vegetables and melons. Early morning the poor and the servants of the rich go to buy. There is much shouting in this market; much loud wrangling. Everybody exactly enjoys it.

After I opened the shop I came often to the bazaars. Ish

mael, of course, could buy threads, needles, pins, even ribbons from a sample, but there was much that I needed to select for myself. Besides, I needed to know what materials were available so I could advise customers who had come to my shop to have gowns made.

On these trips I did not want to see only the fabrics displayed in the bazaars. Soon I was allowed into the back rooms to study the bolts of materials. One day I was looking for a certain fabric which was not to be found anywhere in the bazaar. One seller, more helpful than the rest, took me to introduce me to a man who could get it for me from an importer or from a factory.

The bazaar corridor is bisected by another bazaar corridor which runs at right angles. At the point where the four corridors meet there is a court of ancient beauty. A center fountain shoots a stream of water into the air. There are flowers and brick pavement worn ridgy by the passing of many feet. Facing onto this court are the offices of the wholesalers and importers. It was to one of these magnificent offices that the dealer took me. I was astonished at the beauty of the carpet even in this country of beautiful carpets. The furniture was massive and rich. I had read in my school history that the merchants of the bazaar had had a great influence in politics, especially in the Bast of 1906, and at that time I had pictured the sellers of little wares sitting cross-legged behind their displays as being those who held the power. Now I could see what merchants the history books meant. Although I was eighteen I had never seen this part of the bazaar.

I recognized the very polite man to whom I was introduced as a man who had several times been with his wife in my shop. She was a very feminine, birdlike woman. Do you know the softness of the feathers on a bird's palpitating little throat and on its so delicate breast? This I think, is the softness of the beautiful doll-like women of my country.

"I am pleased to serve you," he said, but in his voice there was the tone of a man speaking to a child, or a woman. I was not surprised. In face and body I am very woman. Even in manners, I think, since that has been my education.

I disregarded the tone of voice and answered his spoken words. Very directly I told him what material I wanted, why I wanted it, what I wished to pay for it, and the value it would be to him if I could recommend his fabrics to my customers.

Slowly the tone in his voice changed and after an hour he was talking to me with the voice a man uses for speaking to men. That is the voice that you hear always in America, so being spoken to in this straight-across way would seem no accomplishment at all to American women. In Teheran—in all of Persia and in other Islamic countries also—woman's place is in the home and her occupations in the home are to bear children, care for them, houseclean, cook, sew, launder. If she is wealthy, servants will do these things but she will manage everything. If she reads, it will be from the Koran or from one of the magazines which have come into Persian life in the last ten years. These magazines write of "important" things like perfume and lipstick, never mentioning politics, economics, or international problems.

If a woman tries to think and expresses an opinion on anything outside of her own tasks, her brothers, her husband, even her sons laugh at her with the curling mouth. In the advanced school a girl's mind is a bowl into which much information is poured. This bowl the girl will empty on examination day.

A woman in Persia shares her husband's bed, not his life.

She cannot discuss politics with him, nor help him to run his business.

The first day that I sat in the luxurious office in the bazaar and talked with this man I entered into a new life. We talked of the silk mills at Chalus which I had visited more than three years before with Sank and Fahti. He spoke of the factories at Behshaber and said they turned out twelve million yards of printed cloth each year. He showed me the very beautiful silk fabrics made at Chalus and the silk stockings that were made there, too.

"There are at least twenty-eight woolen mills and textile factories that I know of. You must go to Isfahan and see for yourself," he said.

I had been to Isfahan but I had not seen for myself.

As I took a taxi back to the shop I felt a strange feeling of well-being. Exhilaration, you say. I wondered why. This broker had given me a beautiful piece of fabric for dressing a mannequin and I had promised to tell women who admired the fabric where it could be purchased. But such gifts had come to me before. Abruptly I put the pieces of the puzzle together. Sitting there in that office for the first time in my life I had been a man. Not a doll, not a drudge, not a woman—but a man.

Many times I talked with this man in my shop or in his office. We discussed the two hundred factories large and small in my country. We talked about public ownership and private ownership. I said that I thought private ownership was best, but he pointed out what had been accomplished by the eight sugar factories, the cement plant, the metal refining plant, the soap, match, cigarette, tea, canned goods, and small arms plants that the government owned and operated. Small firms, he agreed, like those that produced motor pumps, electric welders, machine tools, were better owned by private individuals or corporations.

I learned the meaning of corporations. I got used to speaking of money in great sums. I began to think, in a small way, of course, about sometime having a factory of my own.

Often at home when I heard men discussing political or economic problems I thought of saying something in the conversation, but I never did. In the family I might open my heart to the others, never my head. Ashbage, for example, knew much about the matters in which I had a growing interest, but I never spoke of these things to him. To him I was a woman, Fahri's little sister. Nothing more.

Now, though I was dead tired from the shop, I began to study the economic situation of my country. I found that we exported carpets, lambskins, small arms, dried fruits; that we imported automobiles, trucks, tires, electrical appliances large and small, machinery.

Another day in the bazaar I spoke of these things to the fabric broker. He sighed and put his hands out palms up. "Every day we send out less. Every day we bring in more." I could not tell if he were happy or sad about this until he said, "Iran must dam that outrunning river."

Back in the shop as I draped material on a round Persian lady of wealth to make her look as much as possible like a skinny girl in an American movie, I saw rivers of *rials* flowing out of Persia to pay for all of the luxury things that we were importing. I saw no silver rivers flowing back into Persia. Only a trickle of silver, like a summer stream.

It was after several more weeks of thinking, after reading books and reports, after again talking with my mind-friend, that my dreams began to take shape. Now it seemed to me that all my life had been pointing toward this one dream. Some-day I would start small factories in the villages, factories which could make the things my people need and some besides for export. Every week I was sending dresses made in my shop to Pakistan, to Iraq, to other parts of the Middle East. These were luxury things, but could there not be a market for com-mon things across our borders?

When I spoke about the idea—not as if it were my big dream, but as if it were an objective idea—my friend in the bazaar wrinkled his forehead. "Why the villages?" he asked. "Why not in the cities close to transportation, close to the factories that make materials?"

I thought of the headman's wife in the Azerbaijan village who had said, "Those long, unproductive winter months." But it might sound like an idea that could come only from a woman if I suggested fitting out factories for use just for the winter months. I did not want the condescending tone to come into his voice.

"Village people are lost in the city," I said.

I wanted to say that a fellah away from the soil is like an arm cut from a man. In the soil there are traditions and cus-toms that preserve him no matter what his hardships.

Suppose I had been born a fellah, I thought. Perhaps I am Najmeh, eighteen, coming from the village. My mother is blind from the close work of the rug making in the darkness of the little adobe hut. My father is crippled with great red shining joints in his knees—rheumatism, maybe—from working in the wetness of the rice fields and having no dry clothing to change to. I will do something for my mother and father, I think. I will go to the city where there is work that gives money.

I am dressed in my long cotton pantaloons, a scanty gathered skirt, an old jacket. Over my head is a cotton scarf which takes the place of the veil of twenty-five years ago. In my handkerchief is tied a few pieces of bread, maybe an extra blouse. Best of all, I have sixty cents wound in a rag and fastened to the inside of my clothes.

A simple village girl.

Maybe I go a long way by foot before I come to the railroad. When I do the sixty cents will not buy a place in a passenger train. Maybe, if I use it to bribe an official instead of trying to buy a ticket, I can ride with the animals in the box cars or sit high on top of the baggage in the baggage car. With the animals I will be warm from the warmth of their bodies. With the baggage I shall, perhaps, freeze.

When I reach the city it will be even more beautiful than my dreams. There will be light even though it is night. In the village all is darkness after sundown. A piece of rag stuck into a little dish of grease may give some light in the little huts but outside there is no light at all. Here lights shine from the houses, there are lights on the streets! It is beautiful.

I do not mind sleeping on the street. I have slept on the ground all my life. The next day I gaze at the so beautiful buildings and my heart is bursting with joy. But even now my stomach is crying. I must get something to put into it.

If I am lucky I may get a job in some household. This would be very, very lucky. Then someone would take care of me and I would be tied to new traditions and customs. Maybe I am lucky to get a job in some factory. There I will make maybe seventy-five cents a day and with that I must buy my food, my clothing, and pay for a place to live.

I am accustomed to eating very little except rice, maybe an onion, maybe a little cheese and milk. To buy these will take money. And I must have tea and sugar because in my country people cannot feel happy without tea. What is left from my salary must buy me somewhere a bed.

The hills rise steeply at the back of Teheran. In the sides of these hills the poor have dug out holes—caves—where they find shelter from winter snows. One side is open so the caves are never warm. Before them runs a crazy, dirty, sewage-smelling alley. With the money I make in the factory I can buy the right to share one of these holes with many others. We will sleep side by side on the ground and cook our little food over a smoky fire. I must have some money left over for the bath, because I must be clean, and I must save some for alms, too, if I am to worship at the Imamzadeh.

Perhaps that first night when I am in the city some woman recognizes that I am from the country by my clothing and by the way I stare. "Come with me, dearie," she says very friendly. I have found a friend. I go with her. She is exactly kind. She takes me to the bathhouse. She gives me new clothes. She gives me food at a table that holds fruit and meat and many good things besides. She gives me a place to stay—the best place I have ever had in my life. For the first time in all my days I see a bed. I find it is mine.

It is a little later that I find that the bed will be my place of business. I do not know what to do. I have heard the words of the Koran. But already I owe the woman much money and she can give me to the police if I do not pay it. After a while I do not mind this business. I am used to it. I do not like the sore that comes on my lip. I do not know that this is the first sign of a terrible disease, but I do not like it.

From the fine house of this woman I will go after a time to a less fine house, but still my business will be the same. Now my customers will not be wealthy men, maybe famous in Persia. Then village boys in the army. I am homesick even while I am in their arms. The village was so fresh, so clean.

After a while I am not good even for the soldiers. Dressed in a ragged dress with a frayed shawl over my head, I will crowd with the other beggars, thrusting my chin up and out and looking with syphilitic dimming eyes from under half-closed lids. Something for my stomach, something for my stomach. Nothing matters but something for my stomach. Not honor, not cleanness, not love for any living thing, just something to ease the pain and quiet the frantic thought of dying from hunger. I do not want to live, but now that I am unclean I am afraid to die.

Perhaps had I been a boy I might have done better. I might have gone to the oil wells of Abadan. But in the extraction of oil 847 Persians were working and 2,884 English workmen when I was keeping my shop in Persia. The jobs the Persian men are holding are the very best in Persia. They pay three dollars a day. Each man has held onto his job for at least thirteen years. If he dies a member of his own family will quickly take his place.

Perhaps I could have gone to the fisheries on the Caspian Sea where top wages are a dollar a day and living conditions are very bad.

I might have been lucky as Ishmael was and find good employment with somebody who was interested enough in him to try to teach him how to live the village way in his new city life.

"I do not want anybody to come to the city," I told this fabric broker. "I want to take industry to the village."

Now I saw the look of condescension in his face. He was saying with his smile and with his eyes that I am a foolish woman, sentimental, not shrewd.

I enjoyed the men-minds I met in my business. My thoughts were not pleasant, but dreaming of making things better for my poor people was pleasant. I liked the excitement of the shop and I was proud of my girls, my tailors, and of Ishmael.

But some of the time I was miserable. It is lonely to be what you call a "career girl" in my country. In my days at the advanced school and at the school of the design there were many girl friends. Now these friends were married and had homes and husbands of their own. Even when we were together it was different. They were not interested in a world of ideas, and I was not interested in the fenced-in world of the home.

Once I went on a skiing trip with my brother, his wife, and

another married couple. After the trip my mother said to me, "Najmeh, I think you should not ski again."

"Why?" I asked.

"You were seen talking to a man."

"Mother," I said, "if I wanted to do anything bad would I do it on a field of shining snow with people all about me?"

"It is not good to talk to a man. To be seen talking to a man," Mother insisted.

Sometimes when I wanted to see a picture show, my nephew, Ali, would meet me and take me to the show. But even though he was four years younger than I he already was so tall, so manlike, so mature, that my customers, seeing me with him, would whisper and wonder.

In my heart I was bothered by the need to *look* a good woman though I found it not a bit hard to *be* a good woman.

I enjoyed the visits of my nephew, Amir, and of his friend, our kinsman, Mohammet. Mohammet is somewhat older than Amir, but they have a meeting of the minds. With these two I could talk about the idea.

"I think Najmeh is born again; that she has been in this world twice," Mohammet said, his dark brown eyes reflective as he considered something I was saying. "I think she has learned more than one should learn in eighteen-nineteen years."

I was glad to hear these words, but I knew they were not true. I was nothing, really. I had so much to learn. The shop had taught me much, was teaching me more every day. From my reading I had learned; from the broker of fine fabrics also.

Yet there was much still to learn about my people and their problems. I was just becoming aware of the dependence of Persia—of any nation—on her neighbors. I wondered where I could learn—learn exactly—how to help my poor people.

# · 16 ·

# THE DECISION

BECAUSE I was lonely I went often to the moving picture show. It is my business, I would explain to myself. Tomorrow my customer may want a dress like that worn in the most recent film of Colbert or Grable. It is funny in my country how people see French or Hollywood films and want to copy exactly the clothes and manners of the women on the screen. They do not consider that Persia is another world—that everything is different. What is right in the film may be very poor taste in Teheran. It is fortunate that Persian women do not expose their bodies in public; otherwise they would be wearing evening clothes for teas or for shopping.

Never go to a film in my country on Friday evening. Then the theaters are full to the last wall with melon-seed-cracking people and the pungent smell of oranges rises like perfume when you step in the door. Any other night but Friday—our weekly holiday—you can see the film in comparative quiet.

I wish that I could remember what film I was seeing the night that I made my important decision. The language spoken in these films is English or dubbed-in French and there are printed titles in Persian for those who cannot understand. I was one of those who read the titles! There was in this certain picture a scene in a factory. I do not know whether it was a picture of the terrible sweatshop conditions of some time ago in America or not. But it looked wonderful to me. Many women were sitting at great power machines and the blue jeans were flowing under the needle and out. Why, if we could make blue jeans like that in Persia every person could have a pair—maybe two pairs! And if we could make blue jeans that way why not dresses, and jackets, even underwear.

In a few minutes the scene changed.

Next night I begged Ali to go again to the picture so that I could look further at this wonderful scene. All day as I had watched my girls with their needles, or sewing careful seams on the shop sewing machines, I had thought of those blue jeans coming in a never-ending stream through the machines. That night as I watched the scene again I noticed the clothing of the women, their well-kept hands, their erect backs. These things I wanted for the women of Persia. To Ali I said, "I am going to America. I am going to the United States."

He laughed. He thought I was making a joke. That was just as well. Even when I spoke I knew it would be better if I told my plans to no one until I had them worked out in my own mind.

Now the shop which had been my life began to take only a minor part of my attention. I worked just as hard and fast as ever. I attended to my customers' desires with the same careful thoroughness, but my mind was elsewhere.

I did not want to come to America to find employment in such a factory. That would make a good private dream for a girl who could think of only her own advancement. If I sought such employment I could learn to run the machines,

I could learn much, of course, but there was much else that I would not have the opportunity to learn. I decided it would be better for me to go to America as a student. In some college I could study business administration, rural sociology, American design, maybe factory methods. I know this sounds like quite a combination, but in my dreams any combination seemed possible.

I began to inquire about the arrangements made by my country for students who studied in other lands. I found that the family of the student must make a large deposit with the government—maybe two or three thousand dollars, and must show evidence that it can continue to pay one hundred and seventeen dollars a month for as long as the student is away.

I did not want my mother to have this obligation. If I sold my shop and used all of the money that I had made in it I could, perhaps, finance things until I became well enough acquainted in America to do something for myself.

I made application for admission to Columbia University and to my government for the school arrangement and for my visa.

While I waited to hear from the American university and from my government I was thinking, studying, planning. I knew the suffering of my country. I had seen it. I thought that I knew many things that added to this suffering, perhaps some things that would make it less. But I knew that I was not wise. I had an education meant for women—not for people, not for participating citizens in a democracy. My mother was a most understanding person but she too was a woman. To my brothers and sisters' husbands I was not capable of important thought.

When Reza took the veil from the women's faces he should

have thought of a way to remove the veil from the minds of the men. Through this veil it is most difficult for a woman to penetrate.

Before I left for America I must find out just what would be best for my people so that I might learn of those things. This I had learned in my shop—I had learned it through my own work and through watching my girls—a man or woman is happiest when he is producing something that the world wants. To make something that may be exchanged for the things that he desires gives him that feeling of being worth while which prepares him to live in a democracy. No gift, whether it be from a rich relative, a much-in-love husband or from the government can equal the small thing that one earns himself.

This may seem a very everyday truth to most people but to me it was the basis of my country's need. Maybe I made the matter seem too simple, but I decided that if every man and woman had the opportunity to produce something our domestic problems would be solved. If the man of modern Persia had the magic lamp of Aladdin he would rub it and say, "Genii, give me a chance to earn what I and my family need."

Many people have had the opportunity to feel worth while because they have produced the so-beautiful rugs and inlays, the pierced silver, the enameling, the hand printing of hand-loomed cotton. But actually these things should not be made for sale. Take the carpets, for example. They should be slowly made as a part-time family project and then the carpet should be kept by the family and enjoyed from life-time to life-time. When the carpet is made for sale, the design is chosen to please the customer and the inspiration for beautiful, original design is not there. When the carpet is to be sold the family bends over it until the sight is dimmed and lost. You will laugh—and I guess it is funny—but the unlearned person in my country will not put on glasses until his sight is gone. For him glasses are for the blind and he will squint and strain over his work until he can no longer see; then he will buy the glasses.

Enamel work and metal work take keener sight and wear out the eyes even sooner.

I would not want these crafts to disappear from my country, but they should exist on the same basis as needle point and crocheting do in America. Reza Shah did a fine thing when he established the Institute of Arts and Crafts to revive and preserve the ancient design; but I think we should not consider these things as basic industries.

Maybe I am wrong.

The League of Nations made a survey of my country. This I studied. It recommended that Persia grow aromatic plants and produce perfume. This I think we might do but I know nothing of perfume except how to use it to make me seem even more a woman. It suggested that other plants be raised for food and medicinal oil. The great need, says the survey, is for simple farm tools: hoes, spades, cultivators, steel plows. It is strange, but the rude implements of the fellah seem a part of the fellah life to me. It takes special imagining on my part to see our farmers using any other tools but the iron-tipped stick.

Later, when I crossed America by bus so I could see little by little, I realized how the lack of farm implements and intelligent farming has crippled my country. As we rolled through the Pennsylvania hills I wanted my mother by me to see how really beautiful a friendly, soft, loving countryside can be. And all the way across the country moving toward the West I saw a clean well-fed people, fresh, bright cities, and a land green and heavy with ripening food crops.

You cannot know how it swells the heart to see things growing at they grow in your Middle West! In my country there is a constant battle to push the sand back from the village farm lands, a browning and dwindling of yield if irrigation kanats fail. Such tallness of corn! To me it looked like a forest. I could get completely lost in that brisk, bright-green jungle.

Where would the primitive tools of my country be in a vast farm land like this. I understand what the survey means.

I studied too, the Allen survey. In this I am especially interested because it is about the problems of the fellah. Again and again I had thought when I was visiting the villages that the landlord in Teheran or maybe Isfahan or some other city, drawing his share of the meager crop from the hard-working fellah, was a bad thing; but always I realized that because the farm must have water, and because it takes much money to keep the kanats in repair small farms might be impossible. But in this report I read that co-operatives rather than capital could control the water—that each farmer could own his land and a share in the water.

Already my country is attempting to make more of the fellah landholders. If a man owns his own land his love for it and his pride in it make a little more grow, I think. Just owning something makes him feel more important and more independent in his thought and action.

Recently in the American papers I have read of the locusts in my country. It made me sick inside. What the locusts eat the people will have to hunger for.

I studied carefully, too, the statement of the government

policy, especially the program of Ahmad Ghavan Sultaneh. It sounded so fine, but it would take so much state money, so much time.

But in all my reading I did not come upon my own private plan for my people. I thought of the woman in the Azerbaijan village who said, "Those wasted months of winter." On her words I based my plan.

What I want to do is to establish in the large village or in a small village with other villages in the same area, the little factory. Not the great factory with thousands of humming machines, but the small factory that will employ the women in productive work. I want them to make simple clothing for men, women, children, but especially for women.

In America you can buy a cotton dress for maybe two-ninety-eight. In Persia there is no dress that looks like this. Even the commonest, ugly clothes of the hungry peasant cost many times this amount. With several small factories for the sewing, the price of the dress would be much less and the poor women could have the happiness of looking attractive.

No matter where woman is, no matter how she acts, what her customs are, the heart longs for the same thing—to be told that she is beautiful, that she is loved. A woman is beaten when she is no longer beautiful. How is life for the fellah woman, dressed day and night in the dull, shapeless blue garment of coarse cotton? For her there is the passion of man, but not his admiration, not his proud, caressing eyes, not the words her ears hunger to hear.

To me, almost as great as the need for food is this innate need for personal attractiveness.

My plan which would give women work would also dress them, and I think it would do something more. I think it would make the women know that they are important to their families and to their country, and perhaps after many lifetimes they could make the men feel, too, that women are individuals of value.

I have thought much of the hunger of the poor. The women's earnings in the factory would do much to buy food for the husband and children when there were crop failures. I think now of the farms swept by locusts and no other income in thousands of families. Maybe if this plan really succeeded Zarah could say every night, "I thank God that there is no hunger in Persia."

Remembering the picture of rivers of silver running out of Persia and only a trickle running in, I think of how such factories might change this. All around Persia is an excellent market for inexpensive clothing. Money need not flow out to buy these things and money may flow in if we sell across our borders.

To carry out my plan will take very much money. Perhaps I should start with the money I have saved from my shop, but still I do not know exactly how to begin. I must go to America for the learning. I will put the problem of the money in the lower drawer of my head until I have time for it.

But in spite of my decision to put that problem out of thought, often I considered it. Perhaps I can interest American capital in my plans, I thought.

In Persia the people feel that every American has endless money to invest. The films give such a picture of prosperity. And since I came to America I have had businessmen ask me the details of my plan. When I speak of interesting capital they say, "It sounds like an excellent proposition, but—"

The but, I find, is because of several things that have

happened in the world very recently. First, maybe, is the recent nationalization of the Iranian oil. How can Americans be interested in investing capital where the government at any time may confiscate the properties, or take control of them? Maybe I am not wise, but I think I have the answer. At least one answer. I would not wish to interest capital which did not see my plan as I do. It must make money, of course, but not big money. The idea is to help the people and make money at the same time. Everyone knows about the oil industry—everybody knows how little the Persian people—not the Persian government but the Persian people—have profited by the oil industry. If the industry I plan for my people were set up on a sound basis, guaranteeing to the employed even a small part of the prosperity that American factory workers have, it would never be nationalized. You must know that our government moved to nationalize the oil only after the people had demanded it.

Second, maybe, is the position of Persia against the southern side of Russia. "In China," men tell me, "we poured much American money. Who is using that money now?"

It is not hard to answer that question. The Communists.

Let me tell you about my people. There is much that I do not know, but I do know the hearts of my people. It is only hunger that can make them listen to the Communists. If you are starving what does it matter what hand holds the food? You must take it. Hunger destroys the soul of man. I have never thought that gifts of food would influence the minds of my people. I do know, though, that the opportunity to earn this food would be the best insurance possible against the turning of my country toward communism. Most of Persia dislikes and distrusts Russia. Even during World War II we could not understand why America would make such a friend.

I do not know the future. I cannot say to this man who speaks to me, nor to anyone, that Russia will not come and take. But I know my people. To Russia they will not give.

"Will your government help you?" many ask. I cannot say yes. I cannot say no. Governments change rapidly in my country since we do not have your two-party system but rather a many-party system like that of France, and the premier always depends upon a coalition. I do not know if men, reared in the old traditions of my country, would trust a woman with such an enterprise. Success in my preparation in America may add to my size in the minds of the men in my government. I do not know.

Always I have prayed many words when I went to a sacred shrine, to church, to an Imamzadeh. Now I must really pray. I have a knowledge in my heart of what I want to do. I know that since my desires are good God will help me.

Winter was beginning to break up and the snow had gone from the foot of Mt. Demavend when I told my family of my decision and of the things I had done. Fahri and Fahti and their families were at our home for dinner and after we had eaten we sat in the salon enjoying the warmth of the fire.

"I think I shall go to America," I said. No one spoke so I added, "To study."

Fahri laughed. "Oh, Najmeh!"

"It is not a joke. I am serious."

"No!" she said.

I watched my mother's face. "I really mean to. I have applied for admission to Columbia University and they have accepted me. I have my visa." I handed my mother my papers with my quickly taken picture in one corner.

"What an awful picture," she said. "Who took this?"

"Oh, somewhere," I said. "Twenty-five cents, maybe. You stand in the door. Snap. It is finished." I could understand what she meant about the picture. I had had painted when I was seventeen a very beautiful miniature. I sat for forty-eight hours for that and then the artist used more time to complete it. This girl, looking out from the corner of my papers, looked like the very poor old aunt of the girl in my miniature.

I was glad my mother had spoken of the picture. She was minute by minute getting herself under control to say things that were hard for her to say.

"I think it is good," she finally said. "One year from Teheran will teach you much. Besides, you have been killing yourself at the shop."

I did not reply to the way that she had slipped the words "one year" into the conversation. I didn't say yes or no. Instead I said to myself, "God bless my mother. She is strong!" Recently Mohammet wrote to me, "Congratulations for this mother you have in your life." I thought then that an understanding mother whose education outside the home had been little but who wanted every good thing for her children was the best gift that God could give anyone.

When I was little Mother had often told me and my brothers about the mektab she attended. The class met in the home of the mullah who was the teacher. Mother imitated him. All religious men sit—how shall I say it without showing you? They sit by first kneeling then sitting back so that their hips touch their heels. Mother would sit this way and point to us. "You, mind the children." Then to another place. "You are a big girl, you mind the baby." "You clean the house." Then pointing another place, "You! You are too stupid to help my wife with the small baby. You read Koran."

We would laugh at Mother's story and her conclusion: "If I had been intelligent enough to be stupid I would know more about the Koran."

It was this mother who was saying, "I think it is good that you study in America. May God bless you."

Now that Fahri saw that I was really going to America she cried, "Oh," and her voice was a squeal of excitement, "I've always wanted to go to America!"

Ali asked, "Why America, Najmeh?"

"In America they know what I want to know. Besides, America is halfway around the world. I can see half the world going and the other half coming."

Ashbage looked at me very seriously. There is unusual strength in his even features, in his steady dark eyes. "Najmeh, Little Sister," he said, "you can depend upon me to help you. You need not call upon your mother for money. You may call upon me." Was there ever a better brother-in-law in the world?

"I will have enough from the shop to pay my transportation, to deposit with the government, to take care of me until I can find something to do in America."

He smiled at me. It wasn't the smile of a man to a little sister, it was the smile of one person to another. At that moment I knew that I might have talked with Ashbage as I had with the fabric-broker in the bazaar. He would have understood everything. "You are the proudest woman in the world," he said. Then after a time, "There may be other things I can do besides money. There is a Dr. Harris who is here from

America on an agricultural commission. He has been the president of two universities in America. There are others who can give advice."

"You must learn English," Fahti said. And then they all started to teach me the phrases they knew.

"I have no English." That was the first sentence.

"Thank you. No. Yes." Those were the next words.

Then, "I love you."

"With those words—I love you—I can get myself out of most any situation. Those words are the best," I said.

"With those words you could get yourself into a situation!" Fahri said. "You lucky girl. Here you are going to America to say 'I love you' to everybody and I am stuck at home with this!" And she gave Ali a most fond look. I noticed how much like brother and sister Fahri and Ali looked, both tall and slender and handsome. Fahti, too, is shorter than either Amir or Sijavish, who are already grown men.

In my room Zarah was sleeping on her pallet. Not for a long time had we needed her in our household but now that she was old she came often to our home and stayed overnight or for two-three months. She visited in the same way with Fahri and Fahti and with my brothers. Zarah did not waken and I did not speak to her as I got ready for bed. Zarah would not have been capable of an opinion. She would only have been troubled by the news that I was going to the other side of the world.

The next day I wrote to Mohammet and he replied at once. I did not memorize his letter but among other things he said, "You are not a woman. Anything you want you do for yourself. Anything you desire you get for yourself. You go to America and you'll never hear from me again."

In my heart I wondered if I were surprised at the anger in the letter. His words were the words of any man of my country to a woman who wanted a life of her own. But I was hurt. I was sorry because it had been Mohammet who had said when I opened my shop, "You can do it. I have confidence in you."

Later he came to see me. "I know I am not a woman," I told him. "I am a strange creature whose mind must go before her heart. To me a woman's life seems lacking in many things."

I could see myself sitting in the home of a husband, my greatest worry what to prepare for tea and what to say to the difficult women who came for afternoon after afternoon of yak-yak. I tried to explain my plans, my hope for learning things that would help my people. Of course I was excited by the prospects of the long adventure and of the traveling, but for neither of these reasons would I have given up the shop and gone.

"Always I understand you, but it takes me a little while. After I have time for thinking, I understand. I want the thing that is best for you."

So Mohammet and I were again friends and he was ready to say, "You can do it! I have confidence in you."

What really hurt me most was giving up the shop. There was so much of me in The Flower. My customers had called me Lady Flower, or maybe in English, Miss Flower. In Persia we have for Mr. and Mrs. and Miss different words that denote social position so it is hard, sometimes, to think in English. I had to consider the girls, too, because they not only loved me but depended upon me. They are excellent girls, fine sewers, intelligent, but most of them have had few opportunities and the shop has been school, the outside world, and money for living to them.

At first I thought of renting the shop to some other designer on condition that she employ the girls as long as they wanted to work; but that didn't seem wise. Several times I had gone for two or three days for a rest into some nearby village. When

A lady.

I had returned after so short a time the shop was paralyzed. Slowly a decision formed in my mind.

Every seat in the workroom of the shop was filled. New Year's was approaching, and New Year's is the climax of the costume season. Everybody must have new dress, new coat. New Year's I had all the people from my shop at a party as I had the New Year's before. To each I gave a gift. Later the whole party moved to Fahri's home. This was the farewell party to the girls of The Flower, but they did not know it.

The next day of work I spoke to the most capable girl in the shop, Shamsey, and told her that I was closing the shop to study in America.

"My lady. No, my lady."

There were tears in her eyes and I wondered, for a time, what is this America that I should close my shop.

"Yes," I said. "There is a gift I want to give you. I will give you the name of the shop. I will introduce all the customers to you. I will speak for you to the other girls."

She looked about the shop, so beautiful in its shining whiteness, its pale green furniture, its purple draperies and flowers everywhere. "It is too much. I cannot do," she said, folding and unfolding her hands.

"Take the work of the shop to your home. Take the girls to your home. That way there will be no worry."

"But the sewing machines."

"For you I will make a very special price. Choose what you will need and we will arrange."

At noon when the girls were laughing over their tea in the workroom I went in to talk with them.

"We have done well in The Flower," I said, "because we have all worked together. When I am gone I think—"

"When you are gone!" Sadri, one of the girls with whom I had been especially friendly, cried, "When you are gone!"

Then I sat down with them and told them about the blue jeans flowing under the needle, about my decision to study in America. Finally, "When I am gone you can do best for yourselves by staying together. In the home of Shamsey you can go on making dresses for our customers. Shamsey is capable. She will tell you what to do."

There was no more laughter in the shop. Sadri gave a party

in her home for the girls and me, but there was little laughing at the party. Sadri's was a simple home, but in it there was much love and seven daughters. To each of Sadri's sisters I gave a little doll for remembering.

We took very few orders that last month. I had put in the paper three times that everybody who had dresses or coats, or lingerie made in the shop should come and get it. You know people. They are the same everywhere. I hear much talk of the Oriental mind, the Occidental mind, but maybe I am not mature enough to understand. It seems to me that all are alike. They will order a dress and forget it.

I could not go away with dresses in my shop. "Do you know," Lady Put-it-off would say to a friend, "that little Flower left with my three dresses and a coat! I knew that something was wrong with that shop all the time."

So after I had put the notice in the paper three times I had my mother's car take me from place to place delivering the rest of the dresses.

Then came the bottom dropping out of everything. The equipment in the shop was put up for sale. To my home went the things I had borrowed. Everything else went for selling. Ding, ding, ding, down came the purple draperies and the silver rods. Swush, out went the table and the show cases. Every flower finds a buyer. The shop grows more and more empty and so does my heart. I think of the months I spent getting ready to open the shop. This America! Surely I am one foolish girl.

When the shop stands white and empty I do not want to go by that place. I do go, though, to the home of Shamsey and help her get The Flower started in a little way in her home.

Just the other day I heard from Shamsey. She is married now and still she has the shop. It is good. It is the American way for women to be people as well as wives.

Closing the shop had kept me very busy but there were things I still had to do for myself. There were pressing, cleaning, packing. But most important is the religious celebration.

In my country there is a religious celebration for everything. The going-away celebration was in the home of my mother. Ashbage had invited a very famous mullah to come to give the blessing of departure. Ali, Amir, Sijavish, and the children of my brothers had purchased for me a medal, a Moslem religious talisman, to keep me safe on my travel.

For such a celebration a tray is arranged covered with a beautiful white cloth. On the tray there is a flower, the Koran —small as small and maybe white—and a bowl of water on which one leaf floats.

From my family a very religious woman is chosen to hold the tray. I think that she is second cousin to my mother, but we do not have a word for cousin in my country. Around me is my entire family: my mother, my sisters, their husbands and children; my brothers and their wives and children, and there, too, are all of the relatives of my mother and my father. Family is so important in Persia.

There is The Match, not thinking, maybe, that she was the first to put the idea of traveling into my mind. "Dear, are you really going to another world?" she asks longingly.

Because she has always had magic in her stories, I answer, "What is another world? At nighttime, day is another world. In the daytime, night is another world. There is the world of sleeping dreams and the world of waking dreams."

My kinswoman, dressed in a robe of soft pink, not exactly

Western style, but not Eastern either, comes forward with
the tray. I do not know all the prayers that are in my heart
as I walk toward her. All my life I had wished to travel. Curled
against the knee of The Match I had imagined myself in
faraway places. From the time that Zarah had said, "I thank
God that there is no one hungry in Persia tonight," I had
wanted to do something to lessen the want in my country. As
I grew older, especially after I opened the shop, I often
wondered, What can I do? I am not a farmer. I am not an
industrialist, I am not even a man. And I had prayed and my
mind and heart had captured the idea: *There is nothing too
difficult in life. If you want to do the big thing, the best thing,
and believe God, God will help you. Little by little, even the
humblest man, even a woman, can bring good to my country.*

So now I approach the tray and I can feel my knees shaking
and my heart noisy. I put my hand upon the flower (lay hold
of beauty), kiss the Koran (all beauty comes from God, indeed God is the beginning and end of beauty), and wait while
the kinswoman spills the water from the bowl.

> God keep you,
> God watch you,
> God return you to us.
> You are never alone,
> We pray for you,
> Our prayers go with you.

There I stand alone in the midst of my family. My decision
has made me an island in a river. I will need those prayers
which are going with me, to bridge this river.

At the airport my family is again around me. Mother holds
me close in her arms. "Good-by, dear. I am proud of you."
I feel an unusual veil over her usually expressive voice and

when I look into her face I see that she is crying. "It may be that I shall never meet with you again in this life."

I kiss my mother. I do not cry, but tears are near. I am a lonesome child when leaving my mother.

We are all happy when my nephews cry, "Good-by. Don't come back. Don't come back. Good-by." And Mother must turn to them and say, "Hush. Will you hush!"

I settle into my seat with such a mixture of sorrow and happiness that I do not know which is one and which is the other.

Everyone who is dear to me, all of the ancient Persia that is part of me, will be left behind. But I am going to America where everything that I must know before I can really serve my people waits for my learning.

I am going to America!

1954

FRIENDS IN AMERICA,

M Y STAY with you is over. It is strange that I, who came
to gain special technical knowledge, now feel that it is
much more important to have gained friendship, understanding,
love. Because you have given to me of yourselves I am a part of
you: your minds, your understanding, your ways of being, even
your hearts. I go away but I take you with me always because I
have become one of you.

Before I came I knew the size of the American dollar; now I
know how large is the great American heart. Once my mother
told me, "A friend is one who helps." I was angry and thought
her definition was poor and cynical, for to me "one who helps"
meant "one from whom one can get help."

Now in my maturity I can understand the difference in the
two phrases, a difference which all the peoples who are accepting
help from the open hand of America must also see.

I thank you for your understanding of me and of my people,
for Persia is my heart.

In April I was ill with pneumonia. The two weeks I spent in

bed were my first leisure hours since I began my study in America. I read the book which you are about to lay aside.

Two years ago when we began the book one of us had very limited English, the other, no Farsi at all. As I read I laughed and cried because reading was like living the life again. But with my improved English I found some errors which I would like to correct. *Kavir, sajjadeh, Sa'eed, mohr, tasbih, khorish, kalantar, Ramazan Pezhman* are better spellings than we used.

More important are details which told in my limited English may give a wrong impression. A Moslem place of prayer (p. 16), where the forehead is touched to clay brought from the fields of Kerbela, is not properly called a shrine. The mention of ovens (p. 22) may make you think we have modern ranges. We do not; our ovens are what you call Dutch ovens. There are no Islamic dances (p. 29); our dances are from India or from a Persian period more ancient than the Arab invasion.

People have asked me about the seven S foods of the Persian New Year: vinegar, garlic, sumac, apple, jujube fruit, sebestens, green vegetables. There is S in silver (*Seem*). The fish and the egg symbolize fertility.

Reza Shah did not live in the Gulistan Palace (p. 38) but in a modern one, though ceremonies are still held there. There he received official visitors on New Year's and other visitors at designated times, though it was possible to visit the palace without being received by the Shah. The Peacock Throne was brought from Delhi. (An extra letter in the word changed the throne's homeplace from India to Greece.)

Don't let me confuse you on the calendar. Persia has both a lunar and solar A.H. calendar. Mohammed's birthday, celebrated on the 17th of the month of Rabi'ul Awwal (p. 40); Ramazan, the ninth month in which the main portion of the Koran was revealed (p. 68); and Moharram, the first month (p. 66), are all lunar months difficult to place on the A.D. solar calendar.

The Rosekhaneh is not the flag that marks the place of mourning for the martyred Hossein, but the place itself. The flag? Alam-E-Rowzeh Khani (p. 243).

We have thirty-two letters in our alphabet (p. 49) and it was the Farhangistan that was appointed by Reza Shah to purify Farsi (p. 110). My favorite book shop was the Ibn-E-Sina.

An American book about the religions of the world gives a more colorful picture of a Parsee burial than takes place (p. 136). Though I have never seen such a funeral I am told that the dead of the Parsees are dressed in simple white robes and taken to the top of the Tower of Silence, a round tower with a flat, grated top. There the robes are removed and the body is given to the birds, the sun and the weather.

Alexander the Great (p. 139) was said to have been the son of the Persian Prince who later became Darab Shah, and Dhu'lkarnein should not be translated "with the Golden Horn."

Mohammed's childhood name was Al-Amin (p. 162). There are shrines for only seven or eight of the Imams. Some were buried in secret. The twelfth Imam did not die but will come again when it is the end of the world for us all.

In Teheran (p. 169) a treaty between Russia and Great Britain and Iran was signed in January, 1942. It promised that British and Russian forces would be withdrawn from our country not later than six months after hostilities had been suspended. In November, 1943, when Roosevelt and Stalin and Churchill met in Teheran, the three confirmed this pledge.

I was not right about the Senate being called to consider the grave problem of Russia's refusal to leave. That was the way I remembered it, but I have been told by my older friends that what I remember was a special meeting of the Majlis. The Senate was not called until 1950 and these events took place in 1945. My former teacher was a member of the Majlis from Jahrom.

Perhaps we did not give a clear picture of the beautiful Majlis building (p. 170). The building has four doors, two facing west and two facing east. Over the great door flanked by two lions is a marvelous chronogram. It is the date of the granting of a constitution by Mozaffer-ud-Din-Shah in letters that are equivalent to the numbers. The letters themselves read "ADL-E-MOZAFFER" (The Justice of Mozaffer). Because justice is the ideal of my people to the unlearned the inscription meant, "Now everything is right!"

Haroun-al-Rashid (p. 175) was an Abbassidian king who made his court truly Persian. Mohammed Ali Shah (p. 173) nullified the constitution that his father, Mozaffer-ud-Din-Shah, had granted, but he was overthrown.

The unfortunate girl (p. 181) was a friend of my oldest sister, naturally known to me, but not my contemporary.

At times we have used a wrong title: Shahpur Mohammed Reza Pahlavi (p. 78), Hekmat, Minister of Education (p. 109), Shafaq, expert on international affairs (p. 114), and Ghavum-us-Sultaneh (p. 171).

Perhaps this note will correct in your minds not only our errors due to our imperfect understanding, but also similar errors which appear in other books about my country and my religion written in your language. It is my wish that we can understand each other perfectly—someday.

NAJMEH

# IF YOU ARE PUZZLED

I HAVE tried to tell my story in your language, but sometimes there is no single English word that will take the
place of one of ours. It is difficult to write these Persian words
with the English alphabet. We, too, have an alphabet but our
letters and yours are not equivalent. The best I can do is to
pronounce the word very carefully and write it with the letters
from your alphabet that are nearest the sound. This isn't right,
of course, and you can have no real idea of how the words
sound spoken, but it is the best I can do.

As far as I know, no one has made a standard English spell-
ing of these words. In your books I have seen the name of the
Prophet of Islam written: Mohamet, Mohammet, Mohammed, Mohamed.

Perhaps these words I have listed for you are spelled differently in other books in America. I do not know.

*Allah*, sometimes *Alla*. When the powerful revelation of
the existence of one God who was the God of all people came
to Mohammed, he realized the essence of God but had no

name for Him. Mohammed chose the name Allah, the name of a lesser deity with which the people were familiar. He recognized that the name of God might well be anything else —Jehovah, for example.

*Aush.* Soup. Samples of all the vegetables found in the market and chopped fine and simmered together. To them is added small balls of ground meat, perfectly spiced. If the aush you make today tastes like that which you made yesterday, you are a cook without imagination.

*Farsi.* Speaking exactly, Farsi is the ancient language of the Aryans. Speaking loosely, it is the Persian language of today with its mixture of this ancient language with words of Arabic derivation and Western words necessary in a modern world.

*Haram.* Acts forbidden to Moslems. These acts are the sins which are forbidden to man regardless of the circumstances. The great sins are: idolatry, murder, false charges of adultery, wasting the estates of orphans, taking interest on money, deserting from holy wars, and disobedience of parents. Sometimes adultery and wine drinking are classified as great sins.

The soul that has neglected the vajeb or is guilty of the haram is torn violently from the body and thrown into Hell. In Hell the soul suffers fire and brutal beating. Over him spreads the dreaded sand sores of the desert and he is unclean with the discharge from these sores. And on judgment day that soul will be wiped out utterly, while the souls of the worthy will return to a paradisiacal earth to be happy evermore.

*Hejira.* From Mecca to Medina (Medina means "City of the Prophet") Mohammed and his disciple, Abu Bekr, made a most difficult and dangerous journey. This flight is known as the Hejira. Since it ended on Friday, Friday is the Moslem religious day. It also became year one of the Moslem reckoning. This is year 1370 by the Moslem calendar, since a year composed of twelve lunar months is shorter than your year.

*Horisht.* Gravy, made of many herbs and vegetables flavored with the fowl or meat with which it is served. It is something like your Swiss steak except that the meat retains the character of meat—plump, firm, and juicy.

*Imam.* It is very difficult to define the term Imam without talking, also, of the divisions of the Moslem faith. Imam originally meant "leader in prayer." The Sunnite division of the great church of Islam soon made the Imam the secular as well as the spiritual leader of the community. The Shiites, and I am a Shiite, developed a different idea. A leader of prayer here on earth, the Imam's glory becomes a thousand times greater after his death. We think of the Imams of our faith as Catholics, for example, think of their Saints. One branch of Shiites recognized seven Imams, another recognized four, another nine. The branch to which I belong recognizes twelve. All of the Imams except the last met violent deaths. He disappeared in Samara, near Baghdad, but lives on and will return as the Mahdi, the Guided One, when it is the end of time for us all. The burial places of the Imams are shrines for the worship of Believers.

*Imamzadehs.* Men who gained a reputation for being far better than other men, like the Saints of Catholicism, are called "Sons of Imams," though they are not related by blood to any of the twelve Imams. There are shrines to these good men everywhere in Persia, and the shrines, too, are called Imamzadehs.

*Islam.* Translated the word means submission, and to Mohammed this submission must be not to some little venomous God who could be bribed with the blood of sacrifice, but to the One Great God who is the creator and master over all the world.

*Kalandar,* sometimes *Kalantar.* The kalandar is the chief officer, the headman, of a community. In the small village his responsibilities and powers are small. In a large community he is indeed an important man.

*Kanats,* sometimes *quanats,* sometimes *qanots.* Underground canal systems which have been essential always for the watering of Persian soil. Reza Shah was, for a time, interested in giant dam and canal systems like those in America but the best advisers told him that for Persia kanats were best. Water is not stolen, this way, either by man or by the sun.

*Kishkule.* An oval dish with a handle for carrying it. It is used to carry food, especially for ceremonial purposes.

*Koran.* The Koran is the revelation of God, Himself, and of His plan for salvation. It has also been a code of law and a guide to the correct behavior in all political, social, and international situations. For this latter purpose, not the actual actions expected but the principles by which one should act have been revealed in the Koran.

*Majlis.* The lower house of parliament in Iran, first called as a consultive assembly in 1906. From 1909 to 1925 the Majlis grew stronger and became the vocal expression of the people of Persia. Under Reza Shah the Majlis became an approving body, but with the end of his reign it became a deliberating body much like Western parliaments.

*Makruh.* Acts disapproved for Moslems, such as eating pork, dining with Christians.

*Mektab.* The mektab is a Moslem school for the teaching of the Koran. Students are supposed to learn to read Farsi and Arabic, but in many of these schools the students just memorize the verses from the Koran which the mullah who teaches the school happens to know.

*Minaret.* The minaret is a tall, unsupported tower which symbolizes man's soul, standing alone before God.

*Mohbah.* Acts recommended to a good Moslem. For performing the vajeb and the mohbah, followers of Mohammed can expect to enter into Paradise. On death the soul of a believer is lifted from his body and carried above by a "driver and a witness." Arrived above, the soul sees the ledger in which his life's record has been kept by two angels. If his record is good he then enters Paradise where he is dressed in green silk. (Christians picture pearly gates and streets of gold. To desert people green is a much more comforting color than the harsh shine of gold.) In Paradise one lives without want or the fear of want throughout eternity. Those who know the hard life of my people can understand the longing with which they look forward to this Paradise.

*Moher.* The dish of sand which is the center of a personal shrine. The sand, which is shaped into a picture, is brought from some special Moslem shrine. Moslems do not worship the sand, as some people think. Seeing it helps to bring the mind from everyday things to spiritual things, that is all.

*Moslem.*   A follower of Mohammed, a believer in Islam.

*Mosque.*   A Moslem place of worship whose architecture is characterized by the dome which can now be seen nearly every place in the world.

*Mostahab.*   Acts that are permissible to a good Moslem. In this category fall most of the activities of man.

*Mudakhil.*   The Mudakhil is the consideration obtained for a service or a favor. In business it is something like a commission. In politics it is something like a bribe. In political life it is less and less important since constitutional government in Iran.

*Mullah,* sometimes *mulla.*   The mullah is simply an interpreter of Islamic faith. He may be very humble, dressed in ragged robes and teaching in a tiny mektab; or he may be like Kashani, whose name has appeared often in the news, a religious leader to whom many listen.

*Pishkesh.*   "That which goes before." If a wife prepares an excellent dinner for her husband before she shows him the hat which she has brought home on approval, that is "pishkesh," a preparation of the husband for giving approval to the purchase. The pishkesh differs from the bribe in that it isn't a payment for a favor, but preparation for asking a favor. As for me, I would never use the pishkesh, never.

*Polo.*   The delicious rice eaten by the people of Persia. Nothing is more tasteless than plain boiled rice; nothing better than rice prepared in the Persian manner.

*Rial.* The rial is the standard Iranian coin, as a dollar is stand-ard in America. In 1942 one American dollar equaled 32.68 rials, but ten years later the exchange value of the rial was only about one-tenth of what it had been before the "second front."

There are twenty pennies in one rial. A penny may buy a cabbage; a rial a loaf of bread; forty rials may pay a laborer for a long hard day's work.

*Rosekhaneh.* A black flag announcing that the passion of Ali would be performed in the house where the flag was flown.

*Shah.* King.

*Taspi.* The taspi is the string of prayer beads. Those who worshiped Shiva in India first used the prayer beads and from them the Moslems borrowed the idea. The ninety-nine beads on the string represent the ninety-nine names of God. When the Christians saw the taspi during the crusades they also adopted the prayer beads, calling them "the rosary." The taspi also keeps the mind of him who prays upon his prayers.

*Vajeb.* The obligatory acts of a good Moslem: to keep the fast of Ramazon, to go to Mecca at least once in a lifetime, to pray five times daily, to recite the creed (There is no God but God and Mohammed is His Prophet), and to give alms (one-fortieth of one's total possessions).

Persian names are very different from Western names. Perhaps you would like to know how we say those in this story. In Farsi we do not have the heavy accents of the Western languages. In our names each syllable is pronounced with almost the same stress.

Allah akbar Ăl lä ăk băr
Ali Ă lēe
Amir Ă mēre
Ashbage Ăsh bā gä

Dash-ti-Kavir Dăsh tĭ Kă vēre
Dash-ti-Lut Dăsh tĭ Lŭt

Efaht Ē fäht

Fahri Fäh rēe
Fahti Fäh tēe

Hamadan Hăm ă dăn
Hassan Hă săn
Hoseh Hōs ā
Hussein Who sēen

Iran Ear răn
Isfahan Ĭs fá hăn

Jafa Jă á fäh

Mastaneh Măs tăn ĭ
Matched Mătch ĕd
Meshed Mĕsh ĕd
Moher Mō her
Mosen Mōh zĕn

Nahede Nä hēed
Najafi Nă jă fēe

Najmeh Nadge (to rhyme with badge) mĭ
Naheet Nă hēēt
Nejef Nĕ jĕf

Reza Rēē zäh

Sadii Säh dēē
Safire Să fere
Sank Sănk
Shahriza Shäh rēē zäh
Shikuh She kŭh
Shiites She ītes
Shiraz Shēē räz
Sijavish Sēē yäh vŭsh

Tabriz Tă brēēze
Taspi Tăs pēē
Teheran Tá rän

Zarah Zäh räh

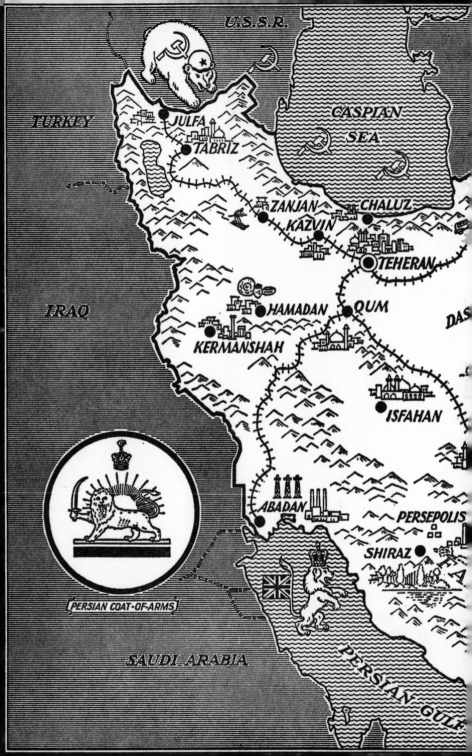

U.S.S.R.

TURKEY

CASPIAN
SEA

JULFA

TABRIZ

ZANJAN

CHALUZ

KAZVIN

IRAQ

TEHERAN

HAMADAN

QUM

DAS

KERMANSHAH

ISFAHAN

ABADAN

PERSEPOLIS

SHIRAZ

PERSIAN COAT-OF-ARMS

SAUDI ARABIA

PERSIAN GULF